1st EDITION

Perspectives on Diseases and Disorders

Lou Gehrig's Disease

Sylvia Engdahl

Book Editor

PERSPECTIVES
On Diseases & Disorders

GALE
CENGAGE Learning

Detroit • New York • San Francisco • New Haven, Conn • Waterville, Maine • London

Elizabeth Des Chenes, *Director, Publishing Solutions*

LIBRARY OF CONGRESS CATALOGING-IN-PUBLICATION DATA

Lou Gehrig's disease / Sylvia Engdahl, book editor.
    p. cm. -- (Perspectives on diseases and disorders)
Includes bibliographical references and index.
ISBN 978-0-7377-5776-7 (hardback)
1. Amyotrophic lateral sclerosis--Popular works. I. Engdahl, Sylvia.
RC406.A24L68 2012
616.8'39--dc23

2011053377

Printed in the United States of America
1 2 3 4 5 6 7 16 15 14 13 12

CONTENTS

Foreword   9

Introduction   11

CHAPTER **1**   Understanding Lou Gehrig's Disease

1. An Overview of Lou Gehrig's Disease (ALS)   16
   L. Fleming Fallon Jr.
   Lou Gehrig's disease is a name often used for
   amyotrophic lateral sclerosis (ALS), a fatal disease
   of the nerves that enable muscle movement, and
   which was virtually unknown until it struck down
   baseball great Lou Gehrig in 1941. Half the people
   who develop it die within three years, and only a
   small percentage live longer than eight years. There
   is no cure, although therapy can help control the
   symptoms. Sooner or later, most ALS patients need
   nursing care.

2. Available Treatments for ALS   25
   National Institute of Neurological Diseases and Stroke
   Only one drug is available to slow the progress
   of ALS, but there is hope that new ones may be
   developed. Other drugs and physical therapy are
   used to alleviate symptoms such as muscle cramps,
   excess saliva, and depression. Gentle low-impact
   exercise can strengthen muscles not yet affected.
   In the late stages of the disease feeding tubes and
   ventilators may be used.

3. Technology Enables People with ALS to Interact with the World   30

Elizabeth Simpson

In the past, people with ALS who could no longer move their limbs or speak could communicate only by blinking. Now computers, voice synthesizers, and other electronic devices enable them to write, talk, read, listen to music, and use the Internet. This is extremely important because ALS affects only muscles, not thought processes; a person's mind remains active.

4. A Genetic Link Between Inherited and Non-Inherited ALS Has Been Found   39

Maria Paul

Researchers have discovered a genetic link between familial (inherited) ALS and sporadic ALS, the cause of which is unknown. They examined the postmortem spinal cords and brains of a hundred patients and found evidence of a particular gene mutation in all those who had either form of the disease. It is hoped that this knowledge may eventually lead to development of a treatment.

CHAPTER 2   Controversies Concerning Lou Gehrig's Disease

1. Some People with ALS Choose to End Their Lives   44

Wendy Johnston

People with ALS have often been central figures in the controversy over legalization of physician-assisted suicide; they are more likely to request it than people with other terminal diseases such as cancer, although few follow through. Doctors should discuss end-of-life issues with patients early, making every effort to preserve their independence and relieve suffering.

2. Lou Gehrig's Disease May Be Caused by
   Blows to the Head   53

   Patrick J. Dobel

   Football players and boxers are stricken with ALS at a
   younger age than the general population, as was Lou
   Gehrig, the baseball player whose name was given to
   the disease. The suggestion has been made that this is
   due to repeated blows to the head frequently received
   in sports. If so, the problem will not go away.

3. Trauma, TDP-43, and Amyotrophic
   Lateral Sclerosis   58

   *Stanley H. Appel, Valerie A. Cwik,
   and John W. Day*

   There is no scientific evidence for the recently
   publicized theory that blows to the head are the
   cause of ALS. An association has been shown only
   by studies that relied on patient recall of head
   injuries; those based on actual records have showed
   no such association. Also, speculation that Lou
   Gehrig had a related disease rather than actual ALS
   is groundless and is misleading to ALS patients.

4. Experimental Treatment with Stem
   Cells May Benefit ALS Patients   65

   Mary J. Loftus

   A clinical trial using stem cells to treat ALS has
   recently begun, its aim being simply to find out
   whether the injection of such cells into the spinal
   cord is safe. Although patients who volunteer are
   not promised any benefit, they participate because
   they consider it their best hope, as well as for the
   sake of people with other diseases who may be
   helped by stem cell research.

5. Experimental Treatment of ALS with Stem
   Cells Is Unethical and Dangerous   70

   Rebecca Taylor

   Media coverage of the trial treatment of ALS with
   stem cell injections does not mention that the fetal
   stem cells used are obtained from aborted fetuses,
   which means it is just as unethical as research using
   embryonic stem cells. Moreover, the experiment is
   dangerous because a boy who was injected with fetal
   stem cells to treat a similar disease developed brain
   and spine tumors.

6. ALS May Be Caused by Severe
   Emotional Repression   75

   Gabor Maté

   Many doctors have noticed that ALS patients tend
   to be nice people, and some believe this is due to
   repressed emotions. In an excerpt from his book
   about the effects of psychological stress on the body,
   a physician examines the lives of three famous people
   with ALS and concludes that, as with other cases he
   has known, the link of ALS to childhood and familial
   emotional repression is not mere coincidence.

7. Exercise May Slow the Progression of ALS   85

   Jane Hurly

   A study done with mice genetically altered to
   produce ALS has shown that exercising the type
   of muscles used for fast bursts of speed can slow
   the progress of the disease. Now clinical trials with
   humans are planned, with the hope that exercise—
   which has previously been thought to make ALS
   worse—will benefit patients by increasing the length
   and quality of their lives.

8. Moderate Obesity May Improve
   Survival in ALS Patients   89

Amber Dance

It has long been known that being underweight
shortens the lives of people with ALS. To the
surprise of researchers, it has now been found
that ALS patients who are somewhat obese live
longer than those of normal weight and that
being overweight though not obese helps to some
extent. A clinical trial is being conducted to find
out whether a high-calorie, high-fat diet will be
beneficial for ALS patients.

9. Statin Drugs Do Not Increase the
   Risk of ALS   94

Catharine Paddock

The Food and Drug Administration found no link
between statin drugs and ALS in an analysis of
data from many clinical trials conducted for other
reasons, even though it had received many reports
of patients who developed ALS after taking statins.
It said that there is no reason for doctors to stop
prescribing statins for lowering cholesterol.

CHAPTER 3   Personal Narratives

1. A World-Famous Scientist Tells About
   His Life with ALS   99

Stephen Hawking

The eminent British physicist Stephen Hawking,
who is the most famous person alive today with
ALS and who has survived for decades longer than
usual for ALS sufferers, tells how he adjusted to the
progression of his illness and how he was provided
with a computer and speech synthesizer that has
enabled him to write scientific papers and to speak.

2. Teenage Couple Faces a Deadly Diagnosis   **106**
Allen G. Breed

Sabrina Parker was only fifteen when she developed the inherited form of ALS, which had killed her mother and grandmother. At first she kept it a secret from her boyfriend, Matt, but once he found out, he was determined to support her. When she was sixteen they had a formal friendship ceremony because it was impractical for them to marry, and Matt was beside her when she died.

3. "Night," from *The Memory Chalet*   **115**
Tony Judt

A writer who is virtually paralyzed by ALS describes how difficult it is to be unable to move when he wants to. It is worst at night, he says, when his nurse is sleeping and he must force himself not to call out for help. But he has learned to divert his mind with thoughts and memories, so that one night at a time, he can cope with his isolation and discomfort.

4. A Woman with ALS Makes a Controversial
   TV Public Service Ad   **121**
Sarah Ezekiel

A television ad intended to raise public awareness of ALS was banned from British television because it was considered too shocking. Its imagery shows a young woman locked in a room symbolic of imprisonment in a dysfunctional body while experiencing violent convulsions. The ALS patient who appeared in it describes its production and her disappointment about the ban.

Glossary   **125**
Chronology   **130**
Organizations to Contact   **132**
For Further Reading   **136**
Index   **140**

FOREWORD

"Medicine, to produce health, has to examine disease."
—Plutarch

Independent research on a health issue is often the first
step to complement discussions with a physician. But
locating accurate, well-organized, understandable medical information can be a challenge. A simple Internet search
on terms such as "cancer" or "diabetes," for example, re-
turns an intimidating number of results. Sifting through the
results can be daunting, particularly when some of the information is inconsistent or even contradictory. The Green-
haven Press series Perspectives on Diseases and Disorders
offers a solution to the often overwhelming nature of researching diseases and disorders.

From the clinical to the personal, titles in the Per
spectives on Diseases and Disorders series provide students and other researchers with authoritative, accessible
information in unique anthologies that include basic
information about the disease or disorder, controversial
aspects of diagnosis and treatment, and first-person accounts of those impacted by the disease. The result is a
well-rounded combination of primary and secondary
sources that, together, provide the reader with a better
understanding of the disease or disorder.

Each volume in Perspectives on Diseases and Disorders
explores a particular disease or disorder in detail. Material
for each volume is carefully selected from a wide range of
sources, including encyclopedias, journals, newspapers, non-
fiction books, speeches, government documents, pamphlets,
organization newsletters, and position papers. Articles in the
first chapter provide an authoritative, up-to-date overview that covers symptoms, causes and effects, treatments,

cures, and medical advances. The second chapter presents a substantial number of opposing viewpoints on controversial treatments and other current debates relating to the volume topic. The third chapter offers a variety of personal perspectives on the disease or disorder. Patients, doctors, caregivers, and loved ones represent just some of the voices found in this narrative chapter.

Each Perspectives on Diseases and Disorders volume also includes:

- An **annotated table of contents** that provides a brief summary of each article in the volume.
- An **introduction** specific to the volume topic.
- Full-color **charts and graphs** to illustrate key points, concepts, and theories.
- Full-color **photos** that show aspects of the disease or disorder and enhance textual material.
- **"Fast Facts"** that highlight pertinent additional statistics and surprising points.
- A **glossary** providing users with definitions of important terms.
- A **chronology** of important dates relating to the disease or disorder.
- An annotated list of **organizations to contact** for students and other readers seeking additional information.
- A **bibliography** of additional books and periodicals for further research.
- A detailed **subject index** that allows readers to quickly find the information they need.

Whether a student researching a disorder, a patient recently diagnosed with a disease, or an individual who simply wants to learn more about a particular disease or disorder, a reader who turns to Perspectives on Diseases and Disorders will find a wealth of information in each volume that offers not only basic information, but also vigorous debate from multiple perspectives.

INTRODUCTION

Amyotrophic lateral sclerosis (ALS), which in the United States and Canada is also called Lou Gehrig's disease, is among the cruelest diseases that exist. It affects a relatively small number of people—about two per hundred thousand, the vast majority of whom are over forty years old—and it is not contagious, but its symptoms are devastating. It causes weakness of the body's voluntary muscles, sooner or later resulting in almost total paralysis. There is no cure, and it is always fatal, usually within less than five years.

The disease attacks nerve cells (neurons) in the brain and spinal cord. Motor neurons, which control the movement of voluntary muscles, deteriorate and eventually die, so that the brain can no longer control muscle movement. The muscles themselves are normal at first, but when they no longer receive messages from the brain, they gradually weaken and deteriorate. Patients lose their ability to walk, to use their hands, to speak, and finally to swallow or to breathe. Death generally comes from respiratory failure or disease.

ALS patients are fully aware of what is happening to them; in most cases their minds remain unaffected. Ultimately they become "locked" in bodies with which they cannot interact with the world. In the past, even before that stage, they often could not communicate except perhaps by blinking their eyes to indicate "yes" or "no." But today there are many technological aids to communication for such patients. People with ALS can now use computer-controlled devices to read, write, and speak. Many can continue to do creative work. The eminent physicist Stephen Hawking, a Cambridge University professor who tells about his life later in this book, has had ALS for nearly fifty years—far longer than is usual—and although he is confined to a wheelchair and is unable to speak without a voice synthesizer, he has written a number of popular books for the public in addition to his scientific papers.

There are many others, less well known than Hawking, who are living full lives despite the unrelenting progress of their illness. Among those whose stories are told at the website of the ALS Association are Rich Brooks, a journalist who writes a humorous column for the *Sarasota Herald-Tribune* in Florida; Nick Scandone, who in spite of paralyzed legs won the Gold Medal in the sailboat racing competition of the Paralympic Games; and Lori Coppola, a former athlete who carried the torch in San Francisco for the 2008 Beijing Olympics only six months before her death.

But the most famous of all ALS victims, at least in the United States, is Lou Gehrig. Gehrig was a Major League Baseball player who played for the New York Yankees from 1923 to 1939, setting many records, including a record for the longest streak of consecutive games played, which stood for more than fifty years. In 1939 he found he could not play as well as before; although he was only thirty-six, his coordination was failing, he was unable to hit home runs, and he even stumbled and fell while running to base. He sought a medical opinion about his condition and was diagnosed with ALS, which at that time was virtually unknown to the public. Realizing that he was no longer an asset to the team, he retired, and July 4, 1939, was proclaimed "Lou Gehrig Appreciation Day" at Yankee Stadium. Ceremonies were held before a crowd of over sixty thousand fans, with gifts and trophies presented to him by celebrities and teammates. It was on this occasion that Gehrig made his widely quoted emotional farewell speech: "Fans, for the past two weeks you have been reading about the bad break I got. Yet today I consider myself the luckiest man on the face of this earth. . . .

I might have been given a bad break, but I've got an awful lot to live for."

Two years later, Lou Gehrig was dead. But the publicity surrounding the effect of ALS on such a well-known sports hero brought it national attention; so much so that it was—and still is—often referred to by his name. His wife dedicated the rest of her life to increasing public awareness about the disease in order to raise funds for research that might lead to a cure. Today, there are several nonprofit organizations focused on that goal, and many people with the disease are committed activists, participating in fund-raising events and sharing their stories with the media. Progress toward a cure, however, has been slow. ALS must compete with more prevalent diseases for funding, and before an effective treatment can be found, its cause—which is so far unknown—must be discovered.

About 10 percent of ALS cases are inherited. The other 90 percent appear sporadically and no one knows why, although genetic predisposition may play a part. Genetic testing can reveal only the inherited form of the disease, and the genes that have so far been identified are not present in most cases. Conversely, not all the people who do carry those genes will develop symptoms, and no way is known to prevent them even in the few known to be at risk. Probably multiple factors are involved; there is an ongoing debate among experts about whether ALS is one disease with many causes, or many separate diseases with different causes.

Not all patients are able to function as well as those who remain mentally, if not physically, active in the world. Some do suffer from a form of dementia, although that is rare. The disease progresses differently in different people, in some cases rapidly, in others slowly. In its late stages full-time caregivers are necessary, and much depends on whether someone in the patient's family is available; if not, the person must go to a nursing home.

Either way, a time comes when a decision must be made about whether he or she wants a feeding tube and, later, a ventilator. When the muscles used for breathing fail, the patient will die without a ventilator, but not everyone chooses to have or stay on one. Once ventilation is begun, it can go on for a very long time when there is no hope of ever being free of the machine, and some people do not wish to live that way, unable to make the slightest movement on their own.

Some, in fact—knowing that they will inevitably die of the disease—prefer not to wait for their condition to deteriorate that far. The situation of ALS patients has figured prominently in the controversy about legalizing assisted suicide and euthanasia. Moreover, there have been a few highly publicized cases in which even where it was not legal, victims of the disease obtained help in taking their own lives.

The vast majority, however, find that, like Lou Gehrig, they have something to live for and that the pleasure taken in such things as family and friends outweighs the loss of the physical activities no longer possible for them. Interestingly, research has shown that healthy people imagine disability to be worse than the disabled themselves perceive it to be. Many ALS patients rate their quality of life as high. And among those not yet near death, there is always hope: hope for better treatments to relieve suffering and hope that someday a cure will be found—if not for them, then for patients in the future.

Understanding Lou Gehrig's Disease

BETTING PROHIBITED

An Overview of Lou Gehrig's Disease (ALS)

L. Fleming Fallon Jr.

Amyotrophic lateral sclerosis (ALS), also known as Lou Gehrig's disease, is a progressive fatal disease involving death of the nerve cells of the brain and spine that control the body's voluntary muscles, explains L. Fleming Fallon Jr. in the following viewpoint. Victims of ALS gradually lose the ability to move most of their muscles, Fallon says, although the involuntary muscles of internal organs are not affected. According to the author, there are two main forms of ALS: familial (inherited) and sporadic; the latter accounts for 90 percent of the cases, and its cause is not yet known. There is no cure for the disease and only one drug that slows its course, so treatment consists mainly of drugs that relieve symptoms plus physical and speech therapy to improve a patient's quality of life.

Fallon is a professor of public health at Bowling Green State University in Ohio.

Photo on previous page. Famed New York Yankees first baseman and record-setting hitter Lou Gehrig (left) died of amyotrophic lateral sclerosis in 1941. The illness would come to be known as "Lou Gehrig's disease." (© Mark Rucker/ Transcendental Graphics/ Getty Images)

Amyotrophic lateral sclerosis (ALS) is a disease that breaks down tissues in the nervous system (a neurodegenerative disease) of unknown cause

SOURCE: L. Fleming Fallon Jr., *Gale Encyclopedia of Medicine*, Farmington Hills, MI: Gale, 2006. Copyright © 2006 by Gale. Reproduced by permission of Gale, a part of Cengage Learning.

that affects the nerves responsible for movement. It is also known as motor neuron disease and Lou Gehrig's disease, after the baseball player whose career it ended.

ALS is a disease of the motor neurons, those nerve cells reaching from the brain to the spinal cord (upper motor neurons) and the spinal cord to the peripheral nerves (lower motor neurons) that control muscle movement. In ALS, for unknown reasons, these neurons die, leading to a progressive loss of the ability to move virtually any of the muscles in the body. ALS affects "voluntary" muscles, those controlled by conscious thought, such as the arm, leg, and trunk muscles. ALS, in and of itself, does not affect sensation, thought processes, the heart muscle, or the "smooth" muscle of the digestive system, bladder, and other internal organs. Most people with ALS retain function of their eye muscles as well. However, various forms of ALS may be associated with a loss of intellectual function (dementia) or sensory symptoms.

ALS progresses rapidly in most cases. It is fatal within three years for 50% of all people affected and within five years for 80%. Ten percent of people with ALS live beyond eight years.

Causes of ALS

The symptoms of ALS are caused by the death of motor neurons in the spinal cord and brain. Normally, these neurons convey electrical messages from the brain to the muscles to stimulate movement in the arms, legs, trunk, neck, and head. As motor neurons die, the muscles they innervate cannot be moved as effectively, and weakness results. In addition, lack of stimulation leads to muscle wasting, or loss of bulk. Involvement of the upper motor neurons causes spasms and increased tone in the limbs, and abnormal reflexes. Involvement of the lower motor neurons causes muscle wasting and twitching (fasciculations).

Although many causes of motor neuron degeneration have been suggested for ALS, none has yet been proven

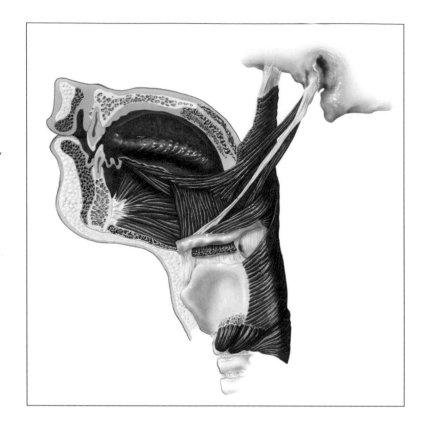

An illustration shows the bulbar muscles in the mouth and throat (in red) that control chewing, swallowing, and speaking. An early sign of ALS is the weakening of these muscles. (© Bo Veisland/ Photo Researchers, Inc.)

responsible. Results of recent research have implicated toxic molecular fragments known as free radicals. Some evidence suggests that a cascade of events leads to excess free radical production inside motor neurons, leading to their death. Why free radicals should be produced in excess amounts is unclear, as is whether this excess is the cause or the effect of other degenerative processes. Additional agents within this toxic cascade may include excessive levels of a neurotransmitter known as glutamate, which may over-stimulate motor neurons, thereby increasing free-radical production, and a faulty detoxification enzyme known as SOD-1, for superoxide dismutase type 1. The actual pathway of destruction is not known, however, nor is the trigger for the rapid degeneration that marks ALS. Further research may show that other pathways are involved, perhaps ones even more important than this one. Autoimmune factors or premature aging may play some role, as could viral agents or environmental toxins.

Two major forms of ALS are known: familial and sporadic. Familial ALS accounts for about 10% of all ALS cases. As the name suggests, familial ALS is believed to be caused by the inheritance of one or more faulty genes. About 15% of families with this type of ALS have mutations in the gene for SOD-1. SOD-1 gene defects are dominant, meaning only one gene copy is needed to develop the disease. Therefore, a parent with the faulty gene has a 50% chance of passing the gene along to a child.

Sporadic ALS has no known cause. While many environmental toxins have been suggested as causes, to date no research has confirmed any of the candidates investigated, including aluminum and mercury and lead from dental fillings. As research progresses, it is likely that many cases of sporadic ALS will be shown to have a genetic basis as well. A third type, called Western Pacific ALS, occurs in Guam and other Pacific islands. This form combines symptoms of both ALS and Parkinson's disease.

Symptoms of ALS

The earliest sign of ALS is most often weakness in the arms or legs, usually more pronounced on one side than the other at first. Loss of function is usually more rapid in the legs among people with familial ALS and in the arms among those with sporadic ALS. Leg weakness may first become apparent by an increased frequency of stumbling on uneven pavement, or an unexplained difficulty climbing stairs. Arm weakness may lead to difficulty grasping and holding a cup, for instance, or loss of dexterity in the fingers.

Less often, the earliest sign of ALS is weakness in the bulbar muscles, those muscles in the mouth and throat that control chewing, swallowing, and speaking. A person with bulbar weakness may become hoarse or tired after speaking at length, or speech may become slurred.

In addition to weakness, the other cardinal signs of ALS are muscle wasting and persistent twitching (fasciculation). These are usually seen after weakness becomes obvious. Fasciculation is quite common in people without the disease, and is virtually never the first sign of ALS.

While initial weakness may be limited to one region, ALS almost always progresses rapidly to involve virtually all the voluntary muscle groups in the body. Later symptoms include loss of the ability to walk, to use the arms and hands, to speak clearly or at all, to swallow, and to hold the head up. Weakness of the respiratory muscles makes breathing and coughing difficult, and poor swallowing control increases the likelihood of inhaling food or saliva (aspiration). Aspiration increases the likelihood of lung infection, which is often the cause of death. With a ventilator and scrupulous bronchial hygiene, a person with ALS may live much longer than the average, although weakness and wasting will continue to erode any remaining functional abilities. Most people with ALS continue to retain function of the extraocular muscles that move their eyes, allowing some communication to take place with simple blinks or through use of a computer-assisted device.

Diagnosis of ALS

The diagnosis of ALS begins with a complete medical history and physical exam, plus a neurological examination to determine the distribution and extent of weakness. An electrical test of muscle function, called an electromyogram, or EMG, is an important part of the diagnostic process. Various other tests, including blood and urine tests, x rays, and CT [computerized tomography] scans, may be done to rule out other possible causes of the symptoms, such as tumors of the skull base or high cervical spinal cord, thyroid disease, spinal arthritis, lead poisoning, or severe vitamin deficiency. ALS is rarely misdiagnosed following a careful review of all these factors.

Treatment of ALS

There is no cure for ALS, and no treatment that can significantly alter its course. There are many things which can be done, however, to help maintain quality of life and to retain functional ability even in the face of progressive weakness.

As of the early 2000s, only one drug had been approved for treatment of ALS. Riluzole (Rilutek) appears to provide on average a three-month increase in life expectancy when taken regularly early in the disease, and shows a significant slowing of the loss of muscle strength. Riluzole acts by decreasing glutamate release from nerve terminals. Experimental trials of nerve growth factor have not demonstrated any benefit. No other drug or vitamin currently available has been shown to have any effect on the course of ALS.

> **FAST FACT**
>
> *Amyotrophic* comes from the Greek: *a* means no or negative, *myo* refers to muscle, and *trophic* means nourishment. *Lateral* ("side") refers to the areas in the spine that undergo *sclerosis* ("hardening"), causing damage to nerves that signal and control muscles.

A physical therapist works with an affected person and family to implement exercise and stretching programs to maintain strength and range of motion, and to promote general health. Swimming may be a good choice for people with ALS, as it provides a low-impact workout to most muscle groups. One result of chronic inactivity is contracture, or muscle shortening. Contractures limit a person's range of motion, and are often painful. Regular stretching can prevent contracture. Several drugs are available to reduce cramping, a common complaint in ALS.

An occupational therapist can help design solutions to movement and coordination problems, and provide advice on adaptive devices and home modifications.

Speech and swallowing difficulties can be minimized or delayed through training provided by a speech-language pathologist. This specialist can also provide advice on communication aids, including computer-assisted devices and simpler word boards.

Nutritional advice can be provided by a nutritionist. A person with ALS often needs softer foods to prevent jaw exhaustion or choking. Later in the disease, nutrition may be provided by a gastrostomy tube inserted into the stomach.

Mechanical ventilation may be used when breathing becomes too difficult. Modern mechanical ventilators are small and portable, allowing a person with ALS to maintain the maximum level of function and mobility. Ventilation may be administered through a mouth or nose piece, or through a tracheostomy tube. This tube is inserted through a small hole made in the windpipe. In addition to providing direct access to the airway, the tube also decreases the risk of aspiration. While many people with rapidly progressing ALS choose not to use ventilators for lengthy periods, they are increasingly being used to prolong life for a short time.

The progressive nature of ALS means that most persons will eventually require full-time nursing care. This care is often provided by a spouse or other family member. While the skills involved are not difficult to learn, the physical and emotional burden of care can be overwhelming. Caregivers need to recognize and provide for their own needs as well as those of people with ALS, to prevent depression, burnout, and bitterness.

Throughout the disease, a support group can provide important psychological aid to affected persons and their caregivers as they come to terms with the losses ALS inflicts. Support groups are sponsored by both the ALS Society and the Muscular Dystrophy Association.

Alternative Treatment

Given the grave prognosis and absence of traditional medical treatments, it is not surprising that a large number of alternative treatments have been tried for ALS. Two studies published in 1988 suggested that amino-acid therapies may provide some improvement for some

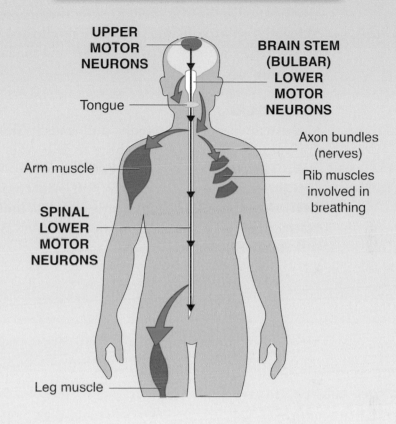

Muscles Affected by ALS

UPPER MOTOR NEURONS

BRAIN STEM (BULBAR) LOWER MOTOR NEURONS

Tongue

Axon bundles (nerves)

Arm muscle

Rib muscles involved in breathing

SPINAL LOWER MOTOR NEURONS

Leg muscle

Taken from: *Facts About Amyotrophic Lateral Sclerosis*, Muscular Dystrophy Association. April 2011. www.als-mda.org/publications/PDF/FA-ALS.pdf.

people with ALS. While individual reports claim benefits for megavitamin therapy, herbal medicine, and removal of dental fillings, for instance, no evidence suggests that these offer any more than a brief psychological boost, often followed by a more severe letdown when it becomes apparent the disease has continued unabated. However, once the causes of ALS are better understood, alternative therapies may be more intensively studied. For example, if damage by free radicals turns out to be the root of most of the symptoms, antioxidant vitamins and supplements may be used more routinely to slow the progression of ALS. Or, if environmental toxins are implicated, alternative therapies with the goal of detoxifying the body may be of some use.

Prognosis

ALS usually progresses rapidly, and leads to death from respiratory infection within three to five years in most cases. The slowest disease progression is seen in those who are young and have their first symptoms in the limbs. About 10% of people with ALS live longer than eight years. There is no known way to prevent ALS or to alter its course.

Available Treatments
for ALS

National Institute of Neurological
Diseases and Stroke

In the following viewpoint the National Institute of Neurological Diseases and Stroke (NINDS) states that only one drug, riluzole, has been approved for treatment of amyotrophic lateral sclerosis (ALS), and it prolongs survival by only a few months. Other treatments merely relieve a person's symptoms, such as fatigue, muscle cramps, and excess saliva, the author says. Physical therapy and gentle exercise can slow the progress of the disease by strengthening unaffected muscles, and speech therapy can help a person to retain the ability to speak as long as possible and, later, to learn to use technological aids for communication. Eventually, states NINDS, patients may choose to use ventilation devices to help them breathe, although this is an option that must be carefully considered in view of its long-term consequences.

NINDS is a member of the National Institutes of Health, the major medical research agency of the US Department of Health and Human Services.

No cure has yet been found for ALS. However, the Food and Drug Administration (FDA) has approved the first drug treatment for the disease—riluzole (Rilutek). Riluzole is believed to reduce damage to motor neurons by decreasing the release of glutamate.

SOURCE: "How Is ALS Treated?," *National Institute of Neurological Disorders and Stroke*, April 15, 2011, www.ninds.nih.gov. Copyright © 2011 by National Institute of Neurological Disorders and Stroke. All rights reserved. Original information has been modified. Reproduced by permission.

Clinical trials with ALS patients showed that riluzole prolongs survival by several months, mainly in those with difficulty swallowing. The drug also extends the time before a patient needs ventilation support. Riluzole does not reverse the damage already done to motor neurons, and patients taking the drug must be monitored for liver damage and other possible side effects. However, this first disease-specific therapy offers hope that the progression of ALS may one day be slowed by new medications or combinations of drugs.

Symptomatic Relief

Other treatments for ALS are designed to relieve symptoms and improve the quality of life for patients. This supportive care is best provided by multidisciplinary teams of health care professionals such as physicians; pharmacists; physical, occupational, and speech therapists; nutritionists; social workers; and home care and hospice nurses. Working with patients and caregivers, these teams can design an individualized plan of medical and physical therapy and provide special equipment aimed at keeping patients as mobile and comfortable as possible.

Physicians can prescribe medications to help reduce fatigue, ease muscle cramps, control spasticity, and reduce excess saliva and phlegm. Drugs also are available to help patients with pain, depression, sleep disturbances, and constipation. Pharmacists can give advice on the proper use of medications and monitor a patient's prescriptions to avoid risks of drug interactions.

Physical therapy and special equipment can enhance patients' independence and safety throughout the course of ALS. Gentle, low-impact aerobic exercise such as walking, swimming, and stationary bicycling can strengthen unaffected muscles, improve cardiovascular health, and help patients fight fatigue and depression. Range of motion and stretching exercises can help prevent painful spasticity and shortening (contracture) of muscles. Physical therapists can recommend exercises that provide these benefits without overworking muscles. Occupational therapists can suggest devices such as ramps, braces, walkers, and wheelchairs that help patients conserve energy and remain mobile.

Speech Therapy

ALS patients who have difficulty speaking may benefit from working with a speech therapist. These health professionals can teach patients adaptive strategies such as techniques to help them speak [more loudly] and more clearly. As ALS progresses, speech therapists can help patients develop ways for responding to yes-or-no questions with their eyes or by other nonverbal means and can recommend aids such as speech synthesizers and computer-based communication systems. These methods and devices help patients communicate when they can no longer speak or produce vocal sounds.

Patients and caregivers can learn from speech therapists and nutritionists how to plan and prepare numerous small meals throughout the day that provide enough calories, fiber, and fluid and how to avoid foods that are difficult to swallow. Patients may begin using suction devices to remove excess fluids or saliva and prevent choking. When patients can no longer get enough nourishment from eating, doctors may advise inserting a feeding tube into the stomach. The use of a feeding tube also reduces the risk of choking and pneumonia that can result from inhaling liquids into the lungs. The tube is not painful and does not prevent patients from eating food orally if they wish.

When the muscles that assist in breathing weaken, use of nocturnal ventilatory assistance (*intermittent positive pressure ventilation* [IPPV] or *bilevel positive airway pressure* [BIPAP]) may be used to aid breathing during sleep. Such devices artificially inflate the patient's lungs

> **FAST FACT**
>
> ALS is not contagious. Only 10 percent or less of cases are the familial, or inherited, form (FALS), and the rest are the sporadic form (SALS), the cause of which is not yet known.

Speech therapists can teach ALS patients adaptive strategies to help them speak more loudly and clearly and, if necessary, to communicate through nonverbal means. (© Hattie Young/Photo Researchers, Inc.)

from various external sources that are applied directly to the face or body. When muscles are no longer able to maintain oxygen and carbon dioxide levels, these devices may be used full-time.

Late-Stage Treatment

Patients may eventually consider forms of mechanical ventilation (respirators) in which a machine inflates and deflates the lungs. To be effective, this may require a tube that passes from the nose or mouth to the windpipe (trachea) and for long-term use, an operation such as a tracheostomy, in which a plastic breathing tube is inserted directly into the patient's windpipe through an opening in the neck. Patients and their families should consider several factors when deciding whether and when to use one of these options. Ventilation devices differ in their effect on the patient's quality of life and in cost. Although ventilation support can ease problems with breathing and prolong survival, it does not affect the progression of ALS. Patients need to be fully informed about these considerations and the long-term effects of life without movement before they make decisions about ventilation support.

Social workers and home care and hospice nurses help patients, families, and caregivers with the medical, emotional, and financial challenges of coping with ALS, particularly during the final stages of the disease. Social workers provide support such as assistance in obtaining financial aid, arranging durable power of attorney, preparing a living will, and finding support groups for patients and caregivers. Respiratory therapists can help caregivers with tasks such as operating and maintaining respirators, and home care nurses are available not only to provide medical care but also to teach caregivers about giving tube feedings and moving patients to avoid painful skin problems and contractures. Home hospice nurses work in consultation with physicians to ensure proper medication, pain control, and other care affecting the quality of life of patients who wish to remain at home. The home hospice team can also counsel patients and caregivers about end-of-life issues.

Technology Enables People with ALS to Interact with the World

Elizabeth Simpson

Technology has made a huge difference in the lives of people with amyotrophic lateral sclerosis (ALS), says writer Elizabeth Simpson in the following viewpoint. Before computers were available, many could communicate only by blinking. Now, using only the muscles left in parts of their bodies such as fingertips, lips, and eyes—or voice commands, for those who can still speak—they can read, send e-mail, and download music, says Simpson. Although the special devices needed are expensive and not always covered by insurance, nonprofit groups often loan them or provide grants for their purchase. Because the disease is progressive, the author says, it is important for a person to think ahead and plan what equipment will be needed in the next stage.

Simpson is a reporter for the *Virginian-Pilot*, a newspaper in Hampton Roads, Virginia.

Andy Eddowes still has muscle enough in his face to wince at the idea of having Lou Gehrig's disease before the age of computers.

SOURCE: Eizabeth Simpson, "Engaging the Mind," *Virginian-Pilot,* December 3, 2006. Copyright © 2006 by Virginian-Pilot. All rights reserved. Reproduced by permission.

The muscle-wasting disease—known in the medical world as amyotrophic lateral sclerosis [ALS]—already has worked its way through the legs, arms and hands of this 46-year-old retired Navy captain, and partway through his voice. But as is the case with most people with the disease, his mind is marvelously intact.

Just through the lingering sensation left in his fingertips and neck muscles he can download and play his favorite music. He can e-mail Navy buddies from the air squadron he once commanded. He can read books and magazines. He can research his disease to find out what comes next, then order equipment that will help him to stay in the game when only his eyes can move.

It's a far cry from what predecessors with his disease were left with in their final stages: Blink once for yes, twice for no.

The disease that afflicts some 30,000 Americans at any given time is a grim one, regularly mentioned in discussions of physician-assisted suicide. But a saving grace of the times is the technology that has unleashed alert minds from paralyzed bodies.

Electronics and computers have kept people engaged with the world, using everything from portable speaking devices to computers operated by eye movement. "Not only has the technology expanded, but the prices have come down, so people can afford devices to talk with their doctors, tell their wives, 'I love you' and their children they're proud of them," says Catherine Easter, the Virginia director for the ALS Association.

In addition, a field called "brain-computer interfaces" is developing in which people can mentally move a computer cursor with a system that measures brain waves, or with a chip implanted within the brain. It may sound like science fiction, but researchers are testing systems in which people paralyzed by ALS, cerebral palsy and brain injuries use thought to operate computers and move robotic arms.

The equipment Eddowes is using today would have seemed revolutionary to people a decade ago, but it will be rudimentary 10 years down the line.

Help from Technology

Although his voice is barely understandable, he continues to have philosophical discussions with friends about politics and the war in Iraq. He's assembling a photographic family history for his 12-year-old daughter, Rachel. And he shares with a reporter the philosophy that has led him through the darkness of his disease.

"The guide I use to make my decisions is something I heard as a kid," he writes in an e-mail. "I think it was a coffee shop advertisement. "Here it is: 'As you ramble through life, brother, whatever be your goal, keep your eye upon the doughnut, and not upon the hole.'"

If you're looking here for a character like the professor in the best-selling book *Tuesdays with Morrie*, an ALS patient who shares evocative, end-of-life lessons, look elsewhere.

"It always looks darkest . . . ," Eddowes says through a voice-generating device, "just before it goes pitch black."

Eddowes is less emotional and introspective, more analytical and problem-solving. He's upbeat, but no Pollyanna when it comes to the disease, which he describes as "death by a thousand cuts."

Here's his computer-typed explanation of the disease: "ALS causes the nerves that control your voluntary muscles to die. And when the nerve dies, the muscle it controls also dies. Voluntary muscles include anything you can control, like your arms and legs, but also your breathing. ALS doesn't affect your brain or memory, only your muscles."

He pulls no punches with the prognosis of this disease, which researchers have yet to fully understand: "Life expectancy for ALS patients averages three to five years from diagnosis. There's no cure."

Comparison of Normal and Wasted Skeletal Muscles

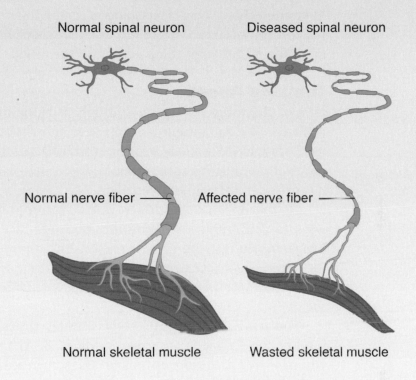

Normal spinal neuron   Diseased spinal neuron

Normal nerve fiber ———   Affected nerve fiber ———

Normal skeletal muscle   Wasted skeletal muscle

Taken from: L. Fleming Fallon Jr. "Amyotrophic Lateral Sclerosis." *Gale Encyclopedia of Medicine*, 3rd ed. Gale, 2006.

But there is technology that can help fill in some of the holes. ALS affects people differently, and at different rates. For some, the voice goes first, but they have muscle enough to click a mouse to communicate. Others can talk but can't move their limbs. For them, voice-recognition devices can allow them to turn on lights and adjust the television volume just by talking.

The disease is a moving target. What helps someone communicate today may not tomorrow, but usually there are adjustments that can be made, or other devices waiting in the wings.

Not all insurance policies cover communication technology—which can cost tens of thousands of dollars—which is why groups like the ALS Association have equipment-loan closets and special grants, not just for communication devices but also for wheelchairs and equipment that helps them get out in the world.

Thinking Ahead

One of the toughest aspects, though, is thinking ahead to make sure equipment is in place to substitute for the next muscle ALS is likely to steal. It's rarely an encouraging exercise. But it's something Eddowes—a planner by nature—cannot help but consider.

On this day in late October, he uses a combination of ways to communicate: Computer messages he's already programmed. Keying in new responses. Snippets of information he's able to relay in the monotone his voice has settled into of late. And Ellen, his wife, who fills in the gaps.

The process is painstakingly slow at times. Nothing like the TV medical show renditions of ALS patients whose words magically appear on the screen within seconds. But it works.

"Rather than worry about the things I couldn't do anymore, I've tried to concentrate on what I could do and on figuring out new ways to continue doing the things I enjoy."

In the dining room of their Virginia Beach home, Ellen places Eddowes' hand, dead weight but for the fingertips, on a mouse attached to a DynaVox speech-generating device mounted before him. "Where do you need your hand?" she asks, adjusting it just so on the mouse. "Is that too high?"

She pulls it down slightly. Eddowes clicks on a panel, and an electronic voice says: "I first noticed ALS symptoms in the fall of 2002, but I didn't know what they were."

The first symptom, he remembers, was a thickening feeling in his throat. In the spring of 2003, he felt weakness in his left hand, followed by random spasms up and down his left arm and side. "Like Christmas tree lights," he says.

He was transferred from Italy—where he commanded an electronic reconnaissance squadron—to Hampton Roads so he could be near doctors at Portsmouth Naval Medical Center. He was about to undergo surgery on his spine when an orthopedist first recommended he see a neurologist in November 2003.

The symptoms were so clear by then, the diagnosis was easy. He took medical retirement from the Navy in April 2005, retiring as a captain after 22 years of service.

FAST FACT

Because ALS is incurable and invariably fatal, the only thing that can be done for its victims is to help them cope with its symptoms.

A year and a half ago he began using a speech-generating device that can be mounted to his wheelchair. By clicking on panels, he can call his dog, Quinto, say, "Good morning," turn on the TV, adjust the volume and talk with others about his care.

When he lost the strength in his arms needed to turn pages of a book, he went online and found a $3,500 device that turns pages. His wife told him that for $3,500, she'd turn the pages for him. So he found a Web site called www.bookshare.org, where he could read books for $75 a year. He's read everything from Harry Potter novels—a passion he shares with his daughter—to [former president] Jimmy Carter's latest book on conflict in the Middle East.

Access to the World

Carlos Urroz is there to help connect the wires to the world. He is an assistive technology manager with the ALS Association and visits more than 300 people with ALS in Virginia, Maryland and Washington [DC]. The computer engineer works in conjunction with speech pathologists, occupational therapists and rehabilitation specialists.

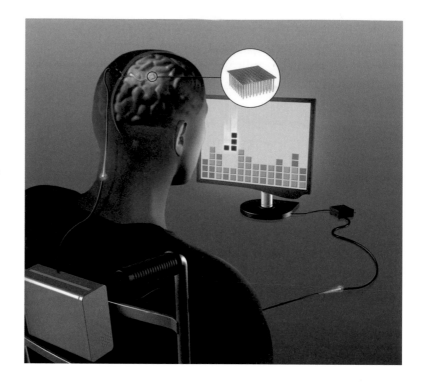

A new field called "brain-computer interface" is emerging that allows ALS patients to communicate through a computer or with a microchip implanted in the brain. (© Claus Lunau/Photo Researchers, Inc.)

Some people prefer low-tech, such as alphabet boards, to spell out words. At the high-tech end are "eye gaze" computers that people can use by looking at the screen to type out letters.

There are all manner of variations in moving a cursor: Some use their cheek or chin or eyebrow, some a "puff and sip" method on a tube. Even if they lose the ability to talk or walk, they can do their banking online. They can get involved in advocacy work. They can read books, magazines, keep up with sports scores and e-mail friends.

"It's like turning on a light sometimes," Urroz says. "Sometimes they were depressed because they weren't interacting with people, they were just looking out the window. The computer becomes their life because it gives them a way to access the world."

It also allows them to weigh in on medical decisions. When their throat muscles become so weak they can't swallow, do they want a feeding tube? As their breathing becomes labored, are they willing to go on a respirator? Once they're on a respirator, is there a point—say when they can no longer communicate at all—when they want to be removed from life support?

It's that point—unable to interact with the world—that health experts refer to as a "locked in state."

A study by German scientists released in the *Psychophysiology* journal in November [2006] found that using computers to engage people with ALS before they reach that point can slow the progression of the disease.

Urroz tries to match people's abilities and interests and comfort levels with devices to keep them engaged, whether it be through a simple gesture or sophisticated electronics. "Any kind of communication keeps the mind active."

Refusing to Give Up

Eddowes has created a haven of sorts in his computer room. He can play [classical composer George Frideric] Handel's "Messiah" or [rock band] Steely Dan or one of hundreds of other songs he's downloaded onto his computer. A tiny patch in the corner of one of the lenses of his glasses is calibrated to an infrared light on the computer that allows him to move a cursor, type messages and surf the Internet. A word-recognition program means he only has to write a few letters of a word and five words pop up. He picks the right one and moves on.

He e-mails friends. He writes letters to raise money for ALS research and organizes trips to Washington to lobby legislators. He downloads photographs and designs scrapbook pages of a family trip out West that he, Ellen and his daughter made while he could still walk.

"I've always enjoyed figuring things out," he writes. "ALS has simply provided me with a whole new realm to attack. . . . I don't view new technology as a surrendering of capability, but as way to maintain capability."

Urroz is already on Eddowes's schedule to return sometime later this month to figure out what devices he needs next because clicking a mouse with his fingertip has become harder. Maybe a sip-and-puff device, or using his cheek or his lip to move the cursor for the day when he can no longer move his head. They'll also talk about technology he can use in a lying down position to prepare for that stage.

There's no easy way out of this disease. "I don't try to pretend that ALS won't get me in the end. I just refuse to give up anything before I absolutely have to. As the flag on the back of my wheelchair says, Don't Give Up The Ship. I've had to give up a great many things so far. But I still have enough that I can do to fill my days and bring some happiness."

One thing about ALS, he says: It gives a person time to think, time to track the doughnut even as the hole gets bigger. He's in this for the long haul. He already has a feeding tube in place for when he can no longer swallow, and he'll let a ventilator breathe for him "when the time comes." But not a moment sooner.

"ALS has changed the way I live," he writes. "I need help doing things like dressing and eating now, but it hasn't changed who I am. And it can't change anything that's already happened in my life. As I see it, ALS only has power over me if I decide to give that power away. And that's something I'll never do."

A Genetic Link Between Inherited and Non-Inherited ALS Has Been Found

Maria Paul

In the following viewpoint Maria Paul says that scientists have so far been unable to discover the cause of amyotrophic lateral sclerosis (ALS). The genes known to be associated with it are found in only 30 percent of inherited cases, and no more than 10 percent of patients have the inherited (familial) form, Paul says. The rest have what is called sporadic ALS, which is of unknown origin. Now, however, researchers have discovered something in common between the two forms of the disease. By testing the spinal cords of postmortem patients, claims Paul, researchers learned that a protein called FUS is present in almost all the ALS cases, but not in cases of people who did not have the disease. This is an important finding, the author claims, because it may lead the way toward an understanding of ALS that might result in an effective treatment for it.

Paul is the health sciences editor at the Northwestern University News Center.

SOURCE: Maria Paul, "Researchers Discover Genetic Link Between Both Types of ALS," Northwestern University News Center, May 5, 2010, www.northwestern.edu. Copyright © 2010 by Northwestern University. All rights reserved. Reproduced by permission.

Researchers from Northwestern University Feinberg School of Medicine have discovered a link between sporadic and familial [inherited] forms of amyotrophic lateral sclerosis (ALS), a neurodegenerative disease also known as Lou Gehrig's disease.

Researchers found that a protein called FUS forms characteristic skein-like cytoplasmic inclusions in spinal motor neurons in most cases of ALS. Mutations in this gene have been previously linked to a small subset of familial ALS cases. Researchers thus linked a rare genetic cause to most cases of ALS, clearing the way for rational therapy based on a known molecular target. The study was recently published online [in 2010] in the *Annals of Neurology*.

The Genetics of ALS

ALS is a disease in which muscle-controlling nerve cells in the brain and spinal cord (motor neurons) die, resulting in rapidly progressive paralysis and death usually within three to five years of the onset of symptoms. Most cases of ALS are of unknown etiology [cause] and appear as sporadic ALS. About 5 to 10 percent of ALS cases are familial. Some forms of familial ALS are caused by genetic mutations in specific genes. Mutations in the Cu/Zn [copper/zinc] superoxide dismutase gene (SOD1) account for approximately 20 percent of familial ALS cases. Mutations in the TAR DNA-binding protein gene (TDP43) and FUS gene occur in about 4 to 5 percent of the familial ALS cases. Altogether, mutations in specific genes have been identified in about 30 percent of familial ALS cases.

In contrast to familial ALS, the etiology and the pathogenic mechanisms underlying sporadic ALS—90 percent of all ALS—has remained largely unknown. Understanding the causes and pathogenic mechanisms of sporadic ALS is the major challenge in this disease.

> **FAST FACT**
>
> ALS is one of the most common neuromuscular diseases worldwide, and people of all races and ethnic backgrounds are affected.

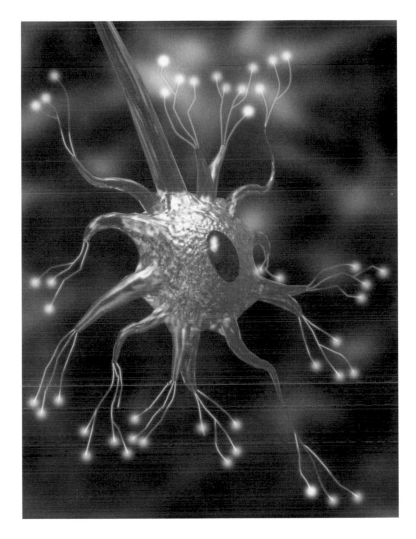

An illustration depicts a motor neuron. When ALS motor neurons die, the result is rapid progressive paralysis and death, usually within three to five years. (© **Alfred Pasieka/ Photo Researchers, Inc.**)

For this study, researchers examined the post-mortem spinal cords and brains of 100 cases, 78 with ALS and 22 in a control group. They found FUS pathology in the spinal cords of all the ALS cases, except for a few cases with SOD1 mutations. But FUS pathology was not present in control cases without ALS.

A Significant Discovery

"This is a game changer because it establishes a connection in the development of sporadic ALS with a known cause of familial ALS," said senior author Teepu Siddique, M.D., the Les Turner ALS Foundation/Herbert C. Wenske Professor of the Davee Department of Neurology and Clinical Neurosciences at Feinberg and a neurologist at Northwestern Memorial Hospital.

"Our finding opens up a new field of investigation for rational therapy for all of ALS," Siddique added. "This is the holy grail of researchers in this field."

"There hasn't been a therapy for most of ALS, because the cause was unknown," Siddique said. "Three genes have been identified in ALS, but the problem has been connecting inherited ALS to sporadic ALS."

"We identified the FUS pathology in sporadic ALS and most familial ALS cases," said Han-Xiang Deng, M.D., associate professor of neurology at Feinberg and lead author of the paper. "The patients with the FUS pathology may account for about 90 percent of all ALS cases. Our findings suggest that pathological interaction of FUS with other proteins is a common theme in motor neuron degeneration in the vast majority of the ALS cases. We believe that this is a major step forward in formulating a common pathogenic pathway for motor neuron degeneration. Importantly, it may offer a novel avenue for developing therapies through targeting these FUS-containing inclusions." The one exception to the new finding is when familial ALS is associated with a mutation on the SOD1 gene. In those patients and in the mutant SOD1 transgenic mouse models, researchers did not find evidence of FUS pathology.

"This tells us that it follows a different pathway of pathogenesis, so treatment for this form of the disease would have to be different," Deng said.

CHAPTER 2

Controversies Concerning Lou Gehrig's Disease

Some People with ALS Choose to End Their Lives

Wendy Johnston

Both medical literature and the media have featured amyotrophic lateral sclerosis (ALS) patients when discussing the controversy over physician-assisted suicide. According to Wendy Johnston in the following viewpoint, there are many possible choices regarding end-of-life issues, yet most patients die without having made an informed choice. Doctors should discuss the options with them early in the course of the disease so that interventions such as the use of ventilators do not occur unless desired by the patient, says Johnston. Whatever type of treatment is chosen, it is essential to make every effort to preserve independence and to relieve suffering, she says.

Johnston is a doctor and an associate professor of medicine at the University of Alberta in Canada.

Photo on previous page. Because athletes are typically stricken with ALS at a younger age than the general population, some experts think there may be a link between concussions, a common sports injury, and ALS. (© AP Images/ Pat Sullivan)

SOURCE: Wendy Johnston, "End-of Life Decision Making In Amyotrophic Lateral Sclerosis," American Academy of Neurology, Treatment of ALS: Controversy and Consensus Seminar, 2005. Copyright © 2005 by American Academy of Neurology. The original article was written by Wendy Johnston, MD, and Cengage Learning has adapted it with permission from the American Academy of Neurology. The American Academy of Neurology has not reviewed nor endorsed, and is not responsible for, any modifications made to the original article.

The controversies surrounding end-of-life decision making in ALS have been featured prominently in both the medical literature and in the general media. Whether in the form of legal appeals, or in televised coverage of actual deaths, patients with ALS have appeared at the forefront of the debate on physician-assisted suicide (PAS) and euthanasia.

The spectrum of apparent choice for patients with ALS ranges from seemingly indefinitely postponing death with long-term assisted ventilation through hastening death by physician-assisted suicide and euthanasia. Regardless of the two extremes, whether by choice or chance, or lack or recourse, most patients with ALS die without availing themselves of either, but as a consequence of disease progression. In the terminal stage, when palliative measures come to the forefront of care, fear of the potential double-effect of using sedatives and painkillers necessary for symptom management, yet that might hasten death, can hamper adequate symptom management at the end of life. . . .

Advance Care Planning

The timing of the discussion of end-of-life issues and advance care planning with patients and their families has to strike a balance between the desire to know on their part, and the need to make timely decisions about life-sustaining therapies. Advance care planning should be considered from the time of diagnosis. In breaking the news about the diagnosis of ALS, planning for interventions should be included as part of disease management, which may lead naturally to discussion of end-of-life issues. . . .

End of life care should be addressed routinely as part of discussions about prognosis, or when considering interventions that could have a low probability of success. More urgent discussions would be prompted by concerns that death is imminent (as perceived by the physician, patient or family) or that disease progression has been severe. An expressed desire to die, queries about assisted suicide and interest in hospice or palliative care must be dealt with immediately. Severe suffering is an emergency that demands medical intervention.

The failure to address advance care planning leads to unplanned interventions. Whether through ignorance or denial, 66% of patients on long-term ventilation (LTV) recently surveyed in Germany were not aware of their impending respiratory failure before emergency intubation and 81% did not give informed consent for the procedure. Although 79% of those on LTV surveyed in six U.S. states were informed about mechanical ventilation, only 21% had chosen it in advance. . . .

Patient autonomy in decision making can only be assured when the available information is presented neutrally, but fully. The resources available to support the decisions must be understood, as well as the family and community support. Advance care planning must be firmly grounded in the values of the individual, who in turn must understand the consequences of the decisions, both for themselves and their family. Values of the individual may not reflect the mainstream; exploring the spiritual and cultural values of the person with ALS and their family should be integral to the decision making process, and should be established before crises occur. When cultural differences appear to preclude patient-centered decision making, or appear at odds with the practitioners, consultation with an institutional ethics committee, community leaders or spiritual counselors of the individual may resolve potential conflict.

Physician-Assisted Suicide and Euthanasia

The re-emergence of the "right-to-die" social movement in the mid-20th century, and its rise to prominence, parallels the development of successful medical interventions to extend life, as well as the legal milestones sanctioning the right of individuals (or their proxy decision makers) to refuse or withdraw life-sustaining measures. Patients with

Triggers for Discussion of End-of-Life Issues with ALS Patients

1. The patient or family asks

2. Severe psychological, social, or spiritual distress or suffering

3. Pain requiring high doses of analgesic medication

4. Dysphagia (difficulty in swallowing) requiring feeding tube

5. Dyspnea (difficulty in breathing), symptoms of hypoventilation (not breathing deeply), or FVC (volume of air that can be blown out) of 50% or less

6. Loss of function in two body regions

Taken from: American Academy of Neurology. "End-of-Life Decision Making in Amyotrophic Lateral Sclerosis." Treatment of ALS: Controversy and Consensus Seminar, 2005. www.alsconnection.org/Johnston,%20W%28 AAN% 29%208BS-006-96.pdf.

ALS have featured prominently in legal challenges, as well as individuals represented in the press and on television.

Patients with ALS seem to be more likely to request and complete assisted suicide or euthanasia than those with other terminal diseases such as cancer. Interest in assisted suicide is high and sustained in Oregon where PAS has been legal since 1998. In a survey of U.S. neurologists, of those that considered themselves specialists in ALS, 41 % had received at least one request for assisted suicide, with two-thirds of requests occurring in the last 6 months of life. Recent studies in New York and Germany indicate a high level of interest in hastening death even in those patients enrolled in a hospice, or under the care of physicians in a palliative care unit.

The debate about the ethics of PAS and euthanasia center on interpretation of basic principles of medical practice that superficially do not conflict: the imperatives to relieve suffering, respect patient autonomy and to do no harm. Medical ethicists have written in support of PAS and euthanasia for patients with ALS and in opposition. It is therefore not surprising that a survey of neurologists reveals a range of attitudes, as well as persistent concerns about the morality and legality of withdrawal of life support and the use of medications that sedate or potentially depress respiratory function.

The American Academy of Neurology and other professional organizations specifically condemn PAS and euthanasia. Yet 44% of neurologists surveyed indicated willingness to perform PAS if legalized, and 13% would do so under current conditions.

In the wake of legalizing PAS in Oregon, studies of the apparent motivation of those requesting or completing PAS suggest that loss of autonomy, control and independence, and the inability to pursue pleasurable activities play a role, more than physical symptoms.

The results of surveys of ALS patients and their caregivers in Oregon and SW Washington also support these core concerns, but in addition, fear of future suffering and higher levels of hopelessness (but not depression) were associated with interest in obtaining a lethal prescription. Fixed characteristics of the individual, including male gender, higher educational and socioeconomic status, and potentially modifiable factors including religiosity were also significantly associated with interest in PAS. There was a mild negative correlation between self-reported quality of life and interest in PAS, but prevalence and severity of physical symptom did not differ significantly between groups. In contrast, a request for PAS in the last month of life did correlate with higher pain scores and insomnia. Interest in, or requests for PAS may reflect a number of concerns. These queries should be approached as the opening to discuss end-of-life issues in general.

The Decision to Hasten Death

An ongoing study of ALS patients in the hospice setting revealed a significant interest in hastening death in 23%. The decision to hasten dying was expressed consistently before death. Those who hastened dying reported poorer mood and less religiosity; they are more likely to have depressive symptoms of clinical significance, feel less in control and more hopeless. Although the numbers are small (11 of 47 deaths were hastened, one by suicide, 10 by sedation for the imminently dying) this careful prospective study is the first to identify factors that might predict interest in hastened death, and factors that may be modified by improved care.

Both PAS and euthanasia have been sanctioned, though only recently legalized [in 2002], in the Netherlands. In the period 1994 to 1999, 20% of patients with ALS, according to the physicians surveyed, died as a result of PAS (3%) or euthanasia (17%). The response of the physicians to the survey was high (responses accounted for 72% of patient deaths). The choice of physician assisted death was positively associated with dying at home, and negatively associated with anxiety and importance placed on religion. Other variables (age, income, educational level, disease or care-related) were not associated with choosing physician-assisted death. "The frequency of feelings of pain, despair, fear, choking and anger were felt to be similar in the two groups of patients" [according to researcher J.F. Veldink]. The study used medical records as well as the physician survey; it is not stated from which source the symptom information was extracted. Two deaths by euthanasia were of unconscious patients who had not explicitly requested it, although one had an advance directive requesting physician assisted death. The study did not directly survey patients, using the physician's recollection and records.

The study by Veldink et al yields other interesting information about death and ALS. No end-of-life decision was made in 54 (27%) of those who died, and in 37 (18%) "such decisions could not be made because the patients

> **FAST FACT**
>
> ALS does not affect a person's ability to see, smell, taste, hear, or recognize touch. Patients usually maintain control of eye muscles and bladder and bowel functions.

died suddenly", although 9/37 had advance directives requesting physician-assisted death. Therefore 40% of patients studied died without having made any decisions. Although tracheostomy [a breathing tube in the throat, considered an "invasive" technique] was present in 3% and NIV [noninvasive ventilation] used in 16% no comment is made about withdrawal of respiratory support nor how such cases were classified. Guidelines for withdrawal of respiratory support from ventilator-dependent patients provide specific recommendations that include both sedation and analgesia, however, it is possible that euthanasia may have been used instead.

In general, requests for assisted suicide and euthanasia do not persist, but persistent requests are very challenging for physicians, even when a legal framework for the query exists. Interviews with physicians in Oregon who received these requests demonstrated that they are emotionally difficult both for physicians who might participate in PAS as well as those who feel they cannot. The physician should be ready to listen thoroughly and assure the patient that no matter what the final decision, the physician is available to the patient through the illness, even if he or she cannot prescribe a lethal medication. Some physicians reported a sense of hopelessness and failure after receiving a request. At other times, too much empathy and identification with the patient will lead to failure to thoroughly look for alternatives. In our experience, patients who persist in wanting assisted suicide have strong needs for control, negative views of the future, and strong dislike of being dependent on others—all areas in which ALS particularly affects patients. There is the risk that too much medical intervention may result in the patient feeling more dependent. Every effort to improve the patient's independence and avoid institutionalization should be made, even if safety in the home is not optimal. . . .

End-of-Life Care

The intensity of symptom management required by many ALS patients in the terminal phase is best supported by hospice services. Symptoms that dominate include excess secretions (saliva, bronchial secretions), dyspnea [difficulty in breathing], insomnia and pain. Hospice also recognizes and supports the caregiver and provides psychosocial and spiritual support for the patient and family. Many have bereavement services as well. It is important to continue to remove barriers to hospice care for ALS patients and their families

The end-of-life decision most frequently made in the Dutch study was the use of medications in doses that "probably shortened the patient's life". Given the context of the study, with categories that reflected the intention of the physician to end life explicitly, this category does not likely reflect intentional overdose, but may reflect concern on the part of the physician that the use of morphine and sedatives such as benzodiazepines would shorten life. Such concerns were reflected in the survey of U.S. neurologists, where 39% equated the use of morphine in treating dyspnea sufficient to depress respiratory drive, with euthanasia. (Moreover, 22% agreed that an intentional morphine overdose was the most humane treatment for terminal ALS.)

Even if pain or dyspnea is acute or severe enough that the doses required could result in clinically relevant respiratory suppression, the prevention of suffering is the more important goal. The principle of "double-effect" refers to such a scenario—when an action can have two morally opposite effects. The criteria used by philosophers and theologians support the use of narcotics and anxiolytic [anxiety-reducing] agents at doses to relieve suffering even at the risk of hastening death. . . .

The best outcome for those with a terminal disease is a "good death", defined by the National Institutes of

[Health] as ". . . one that is free from avoidable distress and suffering for patients, families and caregivers, in general accord with patient and family wishes and reasonably consistent with clinical, cultural and ethical standards". . . .

While interest in PAS may be higher in those with ALS than in other terminal disorders, still, the majority do not ultimately avail themselves of this option even where sanctioned. For most, life is too short, and the struggle to maintain quality of life in the face of disability can be overwhelming. Supportive counseling, informed decision making and aggressive symptom management all have their role in easing the transitions throughout the course of the disease.

Lou Gehrig's Disease May Be Caused by Blows to the Head

Patrick J. Dobel

Lou Gehrig was younger than most people who get amyotrophic lateral sclerosis (ALS), and he had suffered a number of head injuries during his baseball career. According to Patrick J. Dobel in the following article, football players, soccer players, and boxers who have had concussions also are stricken by ALS at a much higher rate than the general population. Some researchers believe that blows to the head create toxic proteins in the brain that cause damage to nerve cells, says Dobel. This is a horrifying discovery since head injuries are unavoidable in professional sports, he claims.

Dobel is a professor of public affairs at the University of Washington and is the school's former faculty athletic representative.

Lou Gehrig lives in life and legend as a classic Achilles figure. He achieved great glory and died young, too young. One of the greatest baseball players of all time, known as the Iron Horse for his relentless play and record setting game streak, he amassed records and respect as the driver of the Yankee dynasty.

Yet at the age of 36 at the height of his career, he was struck with a disease many believed to be amyotrophic lateral sclerosis, ALS. It never made any sense. The disease, which slowly shuts down the organs of the body and still remains largely a mystery, generally strikes people much older and is a death sentence. He died in two years.

[Television journalist] Bryant Gumbel did us all a service with a special report detailing the possible relation between early onset Lou Gehrig's disease and head trauma. Technically Gehrig's disease mimics ALS. The disease involves a progressive shut down of all the body's organs until you die of suffocation. The only organ left untouched is the brain. A person watches in silent horror as his or her body disintegrates piece by piece leaving them with only a mind presiding over a decaying death sentence.

The disease follows an inexorable, fatal and painful course. Its etiology [cause], besides a clear hereditary component [in some cases], has eluded scientists, especially the early opportunistic ALS. Now the research highlighted by Gumbel's team suggests that the same mechanisms that do brain damage to athletes from repetitive head injury may contribute to ALS formation.

> ## FAST FACT
>
> Military veterans, particularly those deployed during the Gulf War, are approximately twice as likely as other people to develop ALS.

Gehrig's Tragic Demise Makes Sense

Suddenly Gehrig's tragic demise makes sense. In a world without batting helmets, he had suffered 6 traumatic head injuries, several of which knocked him out for up to five minutes. Worse, the Iron Horse returned to play the next day after being knocked unconscious. We now know that brain trauma demands total rest of all mental activity, and playing on only aggravates all the neurological damage caused by the accumulation of toxic proteins generated by the concussive blows.

The history of contested data upon concussions and the long-term and short-term impacts on players is still unfolding. After decades of resistance, the football establishment has acknowledged the issue is real, not before hundreds of ex-college and pro football players suffered in silence and penury [poverty] with early dementia, depression, Alzheimer and other illnesses brought on by consistent concussive actions or accumulated head trauma— what is known as chronic traumatic encephalopathy [or] CTE. It took congressional testimony, intrepid reporting by the *Washington Post* and a host of other factors.

Head Injuries Cause Permanent Damage

Gumbel's team detailed the efforts of Dr. Ann McKee, a neurology professor at Boston University, to connect head trauma to this less evident but horrible fate. It turns out that one of the clear effects of concussive trauma upon athletes' brains is the existence of toxic proteins in

At a news conference, Dr. Ann McKee speaks about her discovery that in rare cases concussions can cause toxic proteins to slip through the brain membranes and enter the spinal chord. (© AP Images/Chris O'Meara)

65 year old control   John Grimsley 45 year old ex-NFL player   72 year old boxer

the brain that later infect and impair neural functioning in a wide variety of ways.

Dr. McKee discovered that in rare cases the toxic proteins slip through the brain membranes and enter the spinal cord, the controlling channels for all organ functions. The causal trail is a long ways away, but for the first

Association Between Past Head Injuries and ALS

Country	Number of individuals	Remarks
USA	92 ALS patients.	10 head and/or neck trauma.
Japan	Study A: 712 patients with motor neuron disease (511 with ALS) 637 controls Study B: 158 ALS patients and 158 matched controls.	Previous head injury in 42 patients with motor neuron disease and in 7 controls, mechanical injury (unspecified location) in 48 ALS patients and 27 controls.
UK	63 ALS patients and 61 controls.	Head injury and fractures in 32 patients and 42 controls in the previous 5 years.
USA	135 ALS patients and 85 multiple sclerosis controls.	Head/neck trauma in 31 ALS patients in 13 multiple sclerosis ≥ 1year before onset of disease.
USA	821 head-injured patients.	1 ALS case.
USA	25 ALS and 25 other neuromuscular disease patients.	Severe head, neck, back trauma in 15 ALS patients and in 8 controls.
Italy	143 ALS patients.	9 patients suffered head injury not more than 30 years before disease onset.

Taken from: Ornella Piazza, Anna-Leena Siren, Hannelore Ehrenreich. "Soccer, Neutrauma and Amyotrophic Lateral Sclerosis: Is There a Connection?" Current Medical Research Opinion, 2004. © 2004. www.medscape.com/viewarticle/475273.

time in twenty years of looking, science points towards another horrifying consequence of continuous assault upon the brain. Her team has asked permission to examine the brains and now spinal cords of players who died from ALS. The normal onset of ALS is mid sixties, but European soccer players, American football players and boxers are struck in their thirties and forties and at a rate 10–23 times the normal population.

As I gasped in horror at this story, Gumbel's team interviewed several players (and [their] wives) who faced progressive degeneration from the disease. You could see the stark difference between the player such as Steve Smith, Oakland running back, and what his disease had reduced him to: on a ventilator and speaking through a computer driven by the movement of his eyes.

The story also pointed out how the same statistics and early onset of progressive organ degeneration may be related to CTE in European football, or soccer. There, players regularly whip their heads into balls careening above 60 miles per hour.

The science continues to accumulate and the roster of horrors visited upon football players, American and European, rises. Achilles revenge will strike and the football powers fend off the knowledge by focusing upon concussions as the culprit, when we know it goes far beyond. The problem will not go away, it is woven into the fabric of the sports as seriously as destroying brains is woven into boxing.

Trauma, TDP-43, and Amyotrophic Lateral Sclerosis

Stanley H. Appel, Valerie A. Cwik, and John W. Day

Major periodicals have publicized a theory that repetitive head injuries from playing sports can cause amyotrophic lateral sclerosis (ALS) or an illness like it; some have speculated that Lou Gehrig did not really have ALS. This theory has not been scientifically validated, claim Stanley H. Appel, Valerie A. Cwik, and John W. Day in the following viewpoint. This theory has not been scientifically validated. The research that gave rise to it was based on data from only twelve patients, just three of whom displayed other biochemical indications of ALS, and the proteins found in their spinal cords have also been found in those of people with other diseases, the authors claim. Researchers have been seeking evidence of an association between sports injuries and ALS for decades, and the only studies in which they have found one have been based on patient recall rather than on records. Moreover, state Appel, Cwik, and Day, to imply that Lou Gehrig was misdiagnosed is a disservice to his place in history as well as upsetting to current ALS patients.

Appel is the director of the Methodist Neurological Institute. Cwik is the research and medical director of the Muscular Dystrophy Association. Day is a professor of neurology at the University of Minnesota Medical Center.

SOURCE: Stanley H. Appel, Valerie A. Cwik, and John W. Day, "Trauma, TDP-43, and Amyotrophic Lateral Sclerosis," *Muscle & Nerve*, December, 2010. This material is used by permission of John Wiley & Sons, Inc.

Widespread publicity surrounding a recently published article, entitled "TDP-43 Proteinopathy and Motor Neuron Disease in Chronic Traumatic Encephalopathy," has engendered much consternation from our amyotrophic lateral sclerosis (ALS) patients because media interviews of the authors suggest " . . . brain trauma can mimic Lou Gehrig's disease"—*New York Times*, August 18, 2010, and "Maybe Lou Gehrig Didn't Die of Lou Gehrig's Disease"—*Time* magazine, August 17, 2010. Both statements are lacking in scientific validation. The published study reported on 12 patients with pathological changes of "chronic traumatic encephalopathy (CTE)," 3 of whom had pathological changes of ALS, and claims " . . . that repetitive head trauma experienced in collision sports might be associated with the development of a motor neuron disease." The report was entirely pathological and lacked much clinical information.

What was unique about the pathology in these 3 patients is that two aggregated proteins were noted in spinal cord motor neurons: TDP-43 and tau. TDP-43–positive inclusions have been described previously in many different diseases, including almost all cases of ALS, while tau is also present in many different disorders. The latter is more commonly associated with dementia, but it is far less commonly noted in motor neurons. Aggregated tau is also the pathological hallmark of frontotemporal dementia (FTD), and many familial forms of FTD overlap with ALS.

Based on the findings of both TDP-43 and tau [proteins] in motor neurons of these 3 patients, the authors conclude that the head trauma and chronic traumatic encephalopathy led to the "ALS-like" picture. A more likely explanation is that the patients with clinical evidence of CTE had CTE, whereas patients with clinical evidence of ALS had ALS. Thus, their 3 patients with CTE and ALS most likely had two different diseases, namely, CTE and

ALS. In fact, one of the ALS patients was reported to have a "sibling with probable ALS," suggesting a familial form of the disease. Selective ascertainment of subjects who had both head trauma and a clinical diagnosis of ALS obviously preclude determination by this study of any causal relation between these two conditions.

ALS is diagnosed clinically by the demonstration of symptoms and signs of progressive and relatively selective deterioration of the nerves that control voluntary movement. An expanding list of genetic mutations causes ALS in a minority of patients, but most cases likely result from interaction of genetic and environmental triggers or risk factors, possibly including prior head trauma. These potentially disparate causes may underlie the notable clinical heterogeneity in ALS: the degree of upper and lower motor neuron clinical features differs between patients; the sites of onset can involve limb or speech function; there is a wide range in age of onset and rate of progression; and the degree of cognitive impairment in problem-solving and executive function varies widely. At autopsy, the hallmark of ALS is loss of motor neurons in the brain and spinal cord.

Neuropathological investigations may allow future subcategorization of ALS, but at present the diagnosis of ALS is established by patients meeting the well-defined clinical criteria rather than identification of any stereotypical pathological findings. An additional complexity of the recent article arose when one of the authors, during media interviews, suggested naming the "new" condition in the 3 ALS patients "chronic traumatic encephalomyopathy," or CTEM, even though no clinical or pathological evidence of muscle disease was reported.

The 3 reported cases are too few and too highly selected to prove that CTE can lead to ALS. Clearly, both

CTE and ALS occur separately in most patients; even if they share pathophysiological mechanisms in some individuals, there is no evidence that one condition causes the other.

Professional athletes who succumb to ALS are particularly dramatic and heart-wrenching patients, and a link between ALS and trauma, especially with sports injuries, has been inconclusively sought for decades. Epidemiological studies are still trying to settle the matter. Dr. Lorene Nelson, a renowned neuroepidemiologist at Stanford University, recently commented that " . . . early case-control studies with weak study design features identified physical trauma and skeletal fractures as possible risk factors for ALS. However, one of the pioneers in neuroepidemiology, Dr. Len Kurland, wrote an article in 1992 saying that there was no strong epidemiological evidence of an association. This statement still holds today." In fact, the only studies

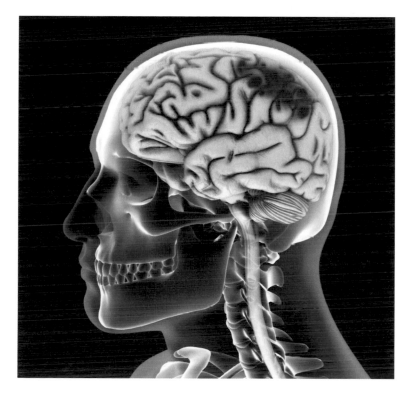

Computer artwork shows, in red, an impact-related head injury. The Muscular Dystrophy Association has reported that, as yet, no link has been found to exist between head trauma and ALS. (© Medi-Mation Ltd/Photo Researchers, Inc.)

Incidence of ALS per 100,000 People at Different Ages

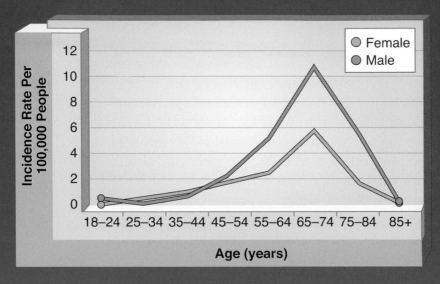

Taken from: G Logroscino et al. "Incidence of Amyotrophic Lateral Sclerosis in Southern Italy: A Population Based Study." *Journal of Neurosurgical Psychiatry*, 2005, vol. 76, pp. 1094–1098.

that have demonstrated a significant association between head injury and ALS are retrospective (case-control) investigations that relied on patient and control subject recall of head injuries; these studies are very susceptible to recall bias. In contrast, records-based studies that did not rely on subject self-report did *not* find any association between head injury and ALS (risk ratios ranging from 0.8 to 1.05). Thus, the totality of evidence does not support the concept that a single head injury or repeated head injuries will lead to an increased risk of ALS. Dr. Nelson and colleagues conducted a rigorous population-based study of ALS in western Washington State that used methods to avoid recall bias, and they did not find an association of ALS with previous fractures, head injuries, or hospitalizations. However, a slightly higher number of fractures was observed in ALS patients compared with controls during the few years preceding ALS diagnosis. This was interpreted as showing that subclinical weakness can increase the risk of falls and fractures early in ALS. This finding has been substantiated by a recent cohort study conducted by scientists in Britain who linked 36 years of hospitalization data (with documentation of head injury) with ALS mortality data. They found that the risk of ALS was only elevated in the first year after head injury, and a similar transiently increased risk of ALS was observed after the occurrence of an arm or a leg injury that required hospitalization. The investigators interpreted these findings as providing evidence that head injury (and limb injury) was most likely to be a "consequence of incipient ALS" that caused an increased tendency to fall.

What is most disconcerting to our ALS patients is the implication that they may have been misdiagnosed. With the extensive media coverage, our patients have been calling, concerned about whether they really have ALS, or something called CTEM. They also want our input as to whether Lou Gehrig really had ALS, especially as the coauthors suggest that Lou Gehrig may have suffered from CTEM rather than ALS. Gehrig was definitively diagnosed with ALS by all the clinical criteria we have noted. What caused his ALS is as unclear today as it was in his time. He clearly had multiple sports injuries, but at no time did he manifest evidence of the cognitive dysfunction characteristic of chronic traumatic encephalopathy. Whether head trauma may have played a role in Gehrig's development of ALS can never be verified, but it is a complete disservice to his place in history as an icon for ALS to suggest that his disease was not ALS. Further studies on the role of TDP-43 and tau as potential therapeutic targets are warranted as are studies of the role of trauma in ALS. In the absence of scientific evidence indicating that CTE causes "an ALS-like syndrome," we must be sensitive to the plight of patients and families who currently confront the ravages of ALS.

Notes

1. McKee AC, Gavett BE, Stern RA, Nowinski CJ, Cantu RC, Kowall NW, et al. TDP-43 proteinopathy and motor neuron disease in chronic traumatic encephalopathy. *J Neuropathol Exp Neurol* 2010; 69:918-929.

2. Cruz DC, Nelson LM, McGuire V, Longstreth WT Jr Physical trauma and family history of neurodegenerative diseases in amyotrophic lateral scierosis: a population-based case–control study. Neuroepidemiology 1999; 18: 101–110.

3. Turner MR, Abisgold J, Yeates DGR, Talbot K, Goldacre MJ. Head and other physical trauma requiring hospitalisation is not a significant risk factor in the development of ALS. *J Neurol Sci* 2010; 288: 45–48.

Experimental Treatment with Stem Cells May Benefit ALS Patients

Mary J. Loftus

As of 2011 a trial of treating amyotrophic lateral sclerosis (ALS) by injecting stem cells into the spinal cord is under way, states Mary J. Loftus in the following viewpoint. The purpose of this first trial is simply to see whether such injection is safe, and no benefit to the subjects has been promised. Nevertheless hundreds of ALS patients applied to be included in the trial, of which only a few were selected; they hope it might slow the progression of their disease or at least help others in the future, says the author. It is thought that stem cells might be able to protect or even revive dying nerve cells in the spine so that they can send messages to the muscles and keep them moving. Stem cell research is controversial, Loftus asserts, because the cells are obtained from human embryos, but advocates point out that those embryos would be discarded anyway and argue that stem cell therapy could save many lives. In any case, the trial now in progress uses fetal stem cells rather than embryonic stem cells.

Loftus is the associate editor of *Emory Magazine*, Emory University's alumni publication.

SOURCE: Mary J. Loftus, "Uncharted Territory: Landmark Stem Cell Trial Offers Hope to ALS Patients," *Emory Magazine*, Spring 2011. Copyright © 2011 by Emory Magazine. All rights reserved. Reproduced by permission.

About six months ago [in the fall of 2010], on the eve of his fifty-ninth birthday, John Conley was preparing to let neurosurgeons at Emory University Hospital inject stem cells into his spinal cord. Conley is one of a handful of patients selected out of hundreds of applicants with amyotrophic lateral sclerosis (ALS) to be part of the first clinical trial in the country to focus on the safety of injecting human stem cells directly into the spinal cord as a possible treatment for ALS, also known as Lou Gehrig's disease.

An expectant grandfather, Conley considers this experimental surgery a gift—not just to himself and his family, on the chance that it might slow the progression of his disease, but to others with neurological diseases who might be helped by advances in stem cell therapies. "Patients like Mr. Conley are agreeing to participate without promise of any benefit. They are doing this to help move science forward," says ALS Center nurse Meraida Polak.

Two years ago, Conley, from Jackson County, Georgia, started experiencing cramps and twitches in his muscles. Although in good physical shape, he began stumbling over things and falling several times a day. He was diagnosed with ALS, a fatal neuromuscular disease. "It just comes on out of the blue, and people start to get weak. They could develop problems with breathing, chewing, swallowing, even speaking," says neurologist Jonathan Glass, director of Emory's ALS Center and principal investigator of the trial site.

FAST FACT

ALS has been 20 percent more common in men than in women, although with increasing age, the incidence of the disease becomes more equal between them, and some reports say that the difference is lessening over time.

Only Testing Safety Now

While this trial tests only whether this treatment is safe, future trials will determine the treatment's effectiveness. ALS affects nerve cells in the brain and spinal cord that control muscle movement; patients usually die within two

How Degeneration of Motor Neurons Affects Muscles

Detailed slice of the spinal cord showing healthy lower motor neurons/muscle on left side and ALS-affected lower motor neurons/muscle on right side.

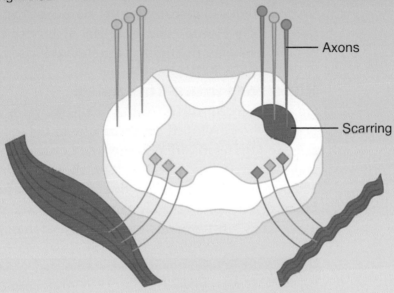

Axons

Scarring

Taken from: Dallas Forshew and Sharon Hulihan. *Living with ALS: What's It All About?* ALS Association, 2007. www.alsa.org/assets/pdfs/brochures/alsa_manual1.pdf.

to five years of diagnosis. About thirty thousand people in the US have the condition and nearly seven thousand are diagnosed each year. No cure exists, and many ALS patient advocacy groups and researchers believe stem cell transplants are the best hope for a therapeutic advance.

But stem cell trials and treatments remain highly controversial. Opponents of this research, including groups such as antiabortion advocates and the Catholic Church, want it to be severely restricted or banned. Proponents, including many medical researchers and patient advocacy groups, say that the embryos (often from fertility or abortion clinics) would be discarded [anyway] and that stem cell research could save countless lives. President Barack Obama signed an executive order last year [in 2010] lifting restrictions on federal funding for embryonic stem cell research. The Georgia Senate approved legislation that would have shut down most forms of embryonic stem cell research in the state, but the proposal failed in the House. The ALS trial at Emory uses fetal neural stem cells, not embryonic stem cells.

Hope for Future Therapies

On October 20, 2010, Emory neurosurgeon Nicholas Boulis, who developed the technique to deliver the stem cells, and his team carefully exposed Conley's spinal cord and delivered five injections—each containing about 100,000 neural stem cells—directly into the bottom of his cord. The spinal cord is extremely delicate, says Boulis, and has low tolerance for any form of manipulation.

An electron micrograph shows fetal blood stem cells. Some experts think that such stem cells might be able to protect—and possibly even revive—dying nerve cells in the spine that send messages to the muscles to keep them active. (© Steve Gschmeissner/Photo Researchers, Inc.)

An associate professor of neurosurgery, he practiced the technique for months on the spinal cords of pigs, which are very similar to the cords of humans.

"We're in uncharted territory here," he said of the surgeries performed on ALS patients. "But I am confident this study is taking therapies for the spinal cord to a new level."

Motor neuron cells begin to die off in individuals with ALS, and the spinal cord isn't able to send messages to muscles, which causes them to atrophy.

"What I'm hoping for is that these neural stem cells will protect the cells that are still there and possibly even allow the sick cells to reconnect with the muscles," Glass says. "We want to keep those muscles moving."

Conley was selected for the surgery in part because he could still walk. The six participants who had their surgeries before him had progressed beyond that level of disease before their stem cell injections. Researchers began the trial with ALS patients who had severe disability (so were at a lower risk for added weakness that might occur as a consequence). They are now moving forward with less disabled patients. The trial participants are being watched closely to see how they tolerate the surgery, the stem cells, and the antirejection medications.

"We have completed eleven patient surgeries, and all are doing well as of this date [spring 2011]," Glass says. "Stopping the disease in its tracks would obviously be the best outcome, but that is a bit of a utopian thought right now. This is just the starting point."

Experimental Treatment of ALS with Stem Cells Is Unethical and Dangerous

Rebecca Taylor

In the following viewpoint Rebecca Taylor argues that the use of fetal stem cells in research is no more ethical than the use of embryonic stem cells, although reports on a 2011 trial of stem cell therapy for amyotrophic lateral scierosis (ALS) patients imply that it is. The fetal stem cells being used, she says, come from aborted fetuses, a fact those reports do not mention. She does not agree with the view that their use is acceptable because the fetus was going to die anyway; it is as bad, she says, as using organs from death-row inmates for transplants would be. Moreover, in her opinion the ALS trial is also dangerous. In the past, a boy with another disease who was injected with fetal stem cells developed tumors in his brain and on his spine. She hopes that researchers will find a better and safer way to treat ALS.

Taylor is a technologist in molecular biology who writes a blog explaining genetics and genetic engineering from a Roman Catholic standpoint.

In all of the controversy over embryonic stem cells, fetal stem cells are often overlooked. What are fetal stem cells? Fetal stem cells come from a fetus anywhere from 8 weeks to 20 weeks gestation. The most common source of fetal stem cells are from aborted fetuses. The use of fetal stem cells in research is often presented as totally uncontroversial. The reason is because fetal stem cells are often called adult stem cells simply because they do not come from embryos.

Do not be fooled. Fetal stem cells are donated by a woman after an elective abortion. In other words, to get fetal stem cells, a fetus must die. This article about the direct injection of fetal stem cells into the spinal cord of a patient with ALS, better known as Lou Gehrig's disease, is a perfect example of how the media often gloss over this fact:

> For the first time in the United States, stem cells have been directly injected into the spinal cord of a patient, researchers announced Thursday.
>
> Doctors injected stem cells from 8-week old fetal tissue into the spine of a man in his early 60s who has advanced ALS, or amyotrophic lateral sclerosis. It was part of a clinical trial designed to determine whether it is safe to inject stem cells into the spinal cord and whether the cells themselves are safe.
>
> ALS is a fatal neurodegenerative disease that causes the deterioration of specific nerve cells in the brain and spinal cord called motor neurons, which control muscle movement. About 30,000 Americans have ALS at any given time, according to the ALS Association.

Neuralstem Inc.

The company that has received FDA [Food and Drug Administration] approval for this trial is Neuralstem Inc. Their website does not announce where they got their fetal stem cells. They could have gotten them from a miscarriage,

Types of Stem Cells Being Used for Research

Type	Source	Advantages	Disadvantages
Embryonic	Embryos (fertilized in vitro)	Can become all cell types of the body. Can be grown easily in laboratories.	Many people believe using them is unethical. There is risk of their turning into cancer.
Fetal	Fetuses (aborted or from miscarriage)	Less frequent ethical objections than use of embryonic cells.	Limited to specific tissue types. Some people believe using them is unethical.
Adult or Somatic	Tissue of a living organism	No ethical objections. Now used for some illnesses to repair tissue from which they come; may become possible to treat other damaged tissue.	Limited to specific tissue types. Difficult to extract and cannot be produced in large quantities.
Cord blood	Umbilical cords	No ethical objections. Similar to bone marrow; can treat diseases of the blood.	Limited to specific tissue types. Not available in quantity.
Amniotic	Amniotic fluid	No ethical objections. Similar to embryonic stem cells.	A recent discovery; so far usable only for research.
Induced pluripotent (iPSC)	Genetically reprogram-med adult stem cells	No ethical objections. Similar to embryonic cells. When patient-specific, no risk of transplant rejection.	A recent discovery; techniques for creating them not yet safe for human use.

Taken from: Compiled by editor.

which would have been an ethical source. The above article also does not mention where the fetal stem cells came from. But a short search brought me to the answer. This press release (taken from Bloomberg.com) clearly states where Neuralstem Inc. got its fetal neural stem cells:

> The researchers used a line of neural stem cells developed by Neuralstem Inc., a closely held biotechnology company based in Rockville, Maryland. The company

developed the line from fetal tissue donated by a woman who underwent an elective abortion at 8 weeks.

The stem cells, taken from an area near the developing spinal cord of the fetus, have the theoretical ability to develop or differentiate into any of three cell types found in the nervous system. The cells were kept alive in culture and chemically manipulated to keep them from differentiating.

Of course the original article about the ALS trial never mentions that the fetal stem cells came from a fetus ripped out of its mother's womb:

> These particular stem cells—which came from the spinal cord of an 8-week-old fetus—are neural stem cells, which have the ability to turn into different types of nerve cells. These are not the same stem cells as the controversial human embryonic stem cells, which destroy the embryo when the stem cells are removed.

It is implied that because these cells do not come from embryos, they are non-controversial. I suppose if you fail to mention that these cells came from an aborted fetus, they fail to stir up controversy. Convenient.

Injected Stem Cells Can Be Harmful

The source of the stem cells is not the only reason to be concerned about this trial. A year ago [in 2009], it was announced that a boy injected with fetal stem cells developed a brain tumor. From the AP [Associated Press]:

> A family desperate to save a child from a lethal brain disease sought highly experimental injections of fetal stem cells—injections that triggered tumors in the boy's brain and spinal cord, Israeli scientists reported Tuesday. . . .

> The unidentified Israeli boy has a rare, fatal genetic disease with a tongue-twisting name—ataxia telangiectasia, or A-T. Degeneration of a certain brain region gradually robs these children of movement. Plus, a faulty immune system leads to frequent infections and cancers. Most die in their teens or early 20s.

Israeli doctors pieced together the child's history: When he was 9, the family traveled to Russia, to a Moscow clinic that provided injections of neural stem cells from fetuses—immature cells destined to grow into a main type of brain cells. The cells were injected into his brain and spinal cord twice more, at ages 10 and 12.

Back home in Israel at age 13, the boy's A-T was severe enough to require that he use a wheelchair when he also began complaining of headaches. Tests at Sheba Medical Center in Tel Aviv uncovered a growth pushing on his brain stem and a second on his spinal cord. Surgeons removed the spinal cord mass when the boy was 14, in 2006 and they say his general condition has remained stable since then.

Many people often argue that using fetal stem cells from an aborted fetus is morally acceptable because the fetus was going to die anyway. The Catholic Church rejects this argument. If an organism must be intentionally destroyed to harvest cells, then the cells are morally tainted. If these fetal stem cells had come from a natural miscarriage, then it would be morally permissible, even laudable, for parents to donate these cells to research. The morality of fetal stem cell use is analogous to that of organ donation. If the patient died of natural causes or a traumatic event, then it is morally permissible to use their organs for the benefit of others. It is not morally permissible to intentionally and prematurely end a person's life and then take their organs for donation. Using fetal stem cells from aborted fetuses is analogous to using organs from death row inmates or victims of euthanasia.

This ALS trial is one to watch. I pray that researchers come up with a better and safer way to treat ALS than the use of fetal stem cells.

FAST FACT

ALS usually does not cause pain except from muscle stiffness and cramping as a result of not moving.

ALS May Be Caused by Severe Emotional Repression

Gabor Maté

Many medical professionals have noticed that amyotrophic lateral sclerosis (ALS) patients tend to be unusually pleasant people. In the following excerpt from his best-selling book *When the Body Says No: The Cost of Hidden Stress*, Gabor Maté argues that this is because typically they repress their emotions. He illustrates this hypothesis by describing the backgrounds of several well-known people with ALS, pointing out that they were emotionally deprived in childhood. In his opinion this is unlikely to be a coincidence, and he believes emotional repression plays a part in causing ALS, although this cannot be proven until scientists have learned more about how the mind affects the body.

Maté is a Canadian physician who specializes in addiction and who believes in a strong connection between the mind and body.

SOURCE: Gabor Maté, *When the Body Says No: Exploring the Stress-Disease Connection*, Hoboken, NJ: Wiley, 2011. Copyright © 2011 by Wiley. Reproduced with permission of John Wiley & Sons, Inc.

"Why Are Patients with ALS So Nice?" was the title of an intriguing paper presented by neurologists from the Cleveland Clinic at an international symposium in Munich [Germany] a few years ago. It discussed the impression of many clinicians that people with Lou Gehrig's disease nearly all seem to "cluster at the MOST PLEASANT end" of the personality spectrum, in contrast to persons with other diseases.

At the Cleveland Clinic, a major referral centre for amyotrophic lateral sclerosis [ALS], the protocol for suspected ALS patients begins with electrodiagnostic testing (EDX). By measuring electrical conductivity, EDX detects the viability or death of motor neurons, the nerve cells that act on muscle fibres. Niceness is commonly perceived by staff to be a feature of the ALS personality, reports Dr. Asa J. Wilbourn, senior author of the paper. His article noted: "This occurs so consistently that whenever the EDX technologists have completed their work and deliver the results . . . they usually accompany it with some comment [e.g., 'This patient cannot have ALS, he (or she) is not nice enough. . . .'] In spite of the briefness of their contact with the patients, and the obvious unscientific method by which they form their opinions, *almost invariably these prove to be correct.*"

"The interesting thing in Munich was that when we presented our paper, everybody came around," says Dr. Wilbourn. "'Oh yeah,' people commented, 'I've noticed that—I've just never thought about it.' It's almost universal. It becomes common knowledge in the laboratory where you evaluate a lot of patients of ALS—and we do an enormous number of cases. I think that anyone who deals with ALS knows that this is a definite phenomenon."

Similar patterns emerge from my personal encounters with ALS patients in private practice and in palliative care. Emotional repression—in most cases expressed as niceness—can also be found on exploring the lives of famous persons with ALS, from the physicist Stephen

Hawking, the baseball great Gehrig, to Morrie Schwartz, the professor whose television appearances on Ted Koppel's show made him a much-admired figure in the last months of his life and whose story and wisdom form the subject of the best-seller *Tuesdays with Morrie*. In Canada, Sue Rodriguez, a person with ALS, gained national prominence with her determined legal battle for her right to assisted suicide. In the end not even a Supreme Court decision could deny her that right. Her story is congruent with what the lives of these others also teach us.

Emotional Deprivation

The life histories of people with ALS invariably tell of emotional deprivation or loss in childhood. Characterizing the personalities of ALS patients are relentless self-drive, reluctance to acknowledge the need for help and the denial of pain whether physical or emotional. All these behaviours and psychological coping mechanisms far predate the onset of illness. The conspicuous niceness of most, but not all, persons with ALS is an expression of a self-imposed image that needs to conform to the individual's (and the world's) expectations. Unlike someone whose human characteristics emerge spontaneously, the individual seems trapped in a role, even when the role causes further harm. It is adopted where a strong sense of self should be—a strong sense of self that could not develop under early childhood conditions of emotional barrenness. In people with a weak sense of self, there is often an unhealthy fusion with others.

> **FAST FACT**
>
> Some ALS patients have a disorder called pseudobulbar affect (PBA), which involves involuntary, uncontrollable crying or laughing spells unrelated to mood. This also occurs in people with other neurological diseases.

The example of New York Yankees first baseman Lou Gehrig is instructive. Gehrig earned the sobriquet "the iron horse" for his implacable refusal to remove himself from the lineup regardless of illness or injury. In the 1930s, long before the days of sophisticated physiotherapy and

Diagnosed with ALS in 1963, noted physicist Stephen Hawking was given only two years to live; as of this writing, he is still living. According to the author, his personality was shaped by intense psychological repression experienced during his childhood. (© AP Images/Markus Schreiber)

sports medicine, he set a record for consecutive games played—2,130—that would stand for the next six decades. He seemed to feel that his prodigious talents and dedicated play when healthy were not enough, and he was too dutiful toward his fans and employers to ever take time off. Gehrig was caught up, according to his biographer, "in his self-designated role as a loyal son, loyal team player, loyal citizen, loyal employee."

A teammate recalled Gehrig's participation in a game despite a broken middle finger on his right hand. "Every time he batted a ball it hurt him. And he almost got sick to his stomach when he caught the ball. You could see him wince. But he always stayed in the game." When his hands were X-rayed, it was found that every one of his fingers had been broken at one time or another—some more than once. Long before ALS forced him to retire, Gehrig had sustained seventeen separate fractures in his hands. "He stayed in games grinning crazily like a macabre dancer in a gruelling marathon," someone wrote. The contrast between Gehrig's unsparing attitude toward himself and his solicitude toward others was glaringly evident when a Yankee rookie was weak from a heavy cold. Placating the annoyed team manager, Gehrig took the young man home to be cared for by his mother, who treated the "patient" to hot wine and put him to bed in her son's room. Lou slept on the couch.

Gehrig has been described as a quintessential "mama's boy." He lived with his mother until his marriage, in his early thirties—a union the mother accepted only with marked ill grace. . . .

Sue Rodriguez

Sue Rodriguez, the Victoria [British Columbia] woman whose court-defying suicide was carried out in the presence of a member of Canada's Parliament, was also emotionally isolated from her family. Her biographer, the journalist Lisa Hobbs-Birnie, describes the day Rodriguez's diagnosis with ALS was confirmed:

> Sue felt her knees buckle, her legs turn to water. She knew what ALS was, had seen the documentary on the physicist-astronomer Stephen Hawking, knew his condition, tried to imagine her own life inside a body that couldn't sit up, walk, talk, laugh, write or hug her child. . . . She leaned against a wall. She became aware of a terrible sound, as primal as the cry of a wounded animal, unlike anything she'd heard before. She realized only slowly, from the horrified expressions of passersby, that it was coming from her own mouth. . . .

> She phoned to tell her mother and step-father, Doe and Ken Thatcher. Doe said: "Ken and I thought it might be that." Sue felt abandoned, and gave way to uncontrollable grief.

Sue was the second of the five children born to her parents within ten years. She was always the outsider. Her mother somehow believed that Sue made this choice: "It almost seemed," she said, "from the moment she was born she didn't feel part of the family in the same way as the others did. The illness only made it worse." Mother and daughter had only occasional telephone contact during the final months of Sue's life. Doe was characterized by her daughter and others as "not the caregiving type."

"The mother's brusque reaction when Sue called from the hospital with her diagnosis," writes Hobbs-Birnie, "was typical not only of Doe's lack of caregiving skill, but of the kind of interaction mother and daughter had. Things did not improve as Sue's disease progressed." Emotional communication was foreign to the Rodriguez family, according to her brother, fourteen months her junior. He was the only sibling to maintain any regular contact with his dying sister. Most of the family, he said, preferred not to show their feelings.

An Excess of Emotion

This is not some bizarre, unfeeling group of human beings here. The problem was not a lack of feeling but an *excess* of painful, unmetabolized emotion. The Rodriguez family dealt with emotional hurt by repressing it. . . .

What drove a terminally ill Sue Rodriguez, the mother of a young child, to expend her diminishing physical and psychic resources on highly public court battles and media campaigns that taxed her vital energies to the limit? An articulate woman with an engaging personality and a beautiful smile, she became a hero to many who saw her as a crusader of indomitable courage and spirit. She was popularly viewed as someone fighting for her right to die at a time and in the manner of her own choosing.

There was always more to the Sue Rodriquez story than the simple issue of autonomy in death, though this was the part of her drama that caught the imagination of

Warning Signs of ALS

ALS generally begins with one or more of the following symptoms. However, they more often indicate other conditions that a doctor must rule out in order to diagnose it. They rarely mean ALS in a person younger than forty.

- Abnormal fatigue of arms and/or legs
- Weakness of one arm or leg
- Dropping things frequently
- Frequent tripping or stumbling
- Foot drop (difficulty raising the foot)
- Fasciculations (muscle twitches)
- Unexplained muscle cramps
- Slurred speech
- Difficulty swallowing

Taken from: Compiled by editor.

the public. Behind the popular facade of a confident and determined fighter, Ms. Rodriguez was a frightened and lonely person with a very fragile support system, alienated from her estranged husband and from her family. . . .

When Sue Rodriguez was diagnosed with ALS, in her first despair she compared the impossibility of her situation with what she perceived were the relative advantages of fellow ALS sufferer Stephen Hawking. Writes Hobbs-Birnie, "She was given pamphlets on palliative care, and these pamphlets described patients who were 'surrounded by loving family' or who found joy in 'living a life of the mind.' What loving family? she thought. What life of the mind? Let a genius like Stephen Hawking live a life of the mind. But me, if I cannot move my own body, I have no life."

Stephen Hawking

If Stephen Hawking's public status as a latter-day [Albert] Einstein may be questioned by science cognoscenti, no one disputes his brilliance, originality of thought or intellectual fearlessness. There is universal admiration for the indomitable will that has sustained his life and work since a slight speech impediment signalled the onset of amyotrophic lateral sclerosis when he was only twenty years old. Diagnosed in 1963, Hawking was given the medical prognosis that he had, at most, two years to live. He has been near death on at least one occasion, ill with pneumonia and in a coma on a trip to Switzerland. Yet four decades after his diagnosis, paralyzed, wheelchair bound and completely dependent physically, he has, nonetheless, just published his second best-selling book. He has travelled ceaselessly around the world, a lecturer in great demand despite his inability to utter a word in his own voice. He has been the recipient of many scientific honours.

Although there are exceptions, the course of ALS is generally predictable. The vast majority of patients die within ten years of diagnosis, many much sooner. Very rarely people do make recovery from what seems like ALS, but it is extremely unusual for a person to live with its ravages for as long as Stephen Hawking has, continuing not only to work but to function at a high level. What has enabled him to confound medical opinion and those grim statistics?

We cannot understand Hawking's course as an isolated clinical phenomenon, separated from the circumstances of his life and relationships. His longevity is, without doubt, a tribute to his spirited determination not to allow the disease to defeat him. But I also believe that Sue Rodriguez's bitter comparison was correct: the young Stephen had access to invisible resources denied to most people with ALS. Given the nature of ALS as a disease that destroys body while leaving the intellect intact, an abstract thinker was in an ideal position to "live a life of the mind.". . . Hawking did not see his body's deterioration as impairing the role that he chose for himself. On the contrary, it may have enhanced it. Prior to his diagnosis and its attendant debility, he had been somewhat aimless, his shining intellectual gifts notwithstanding.

Uncomfortable in His Body

Hawking had always possessed tremendous cognitive and mathematical capacities and confidence, but he never seemed to feel comfortable in his body. "He was eccentric and awkward, skinny and puny," write Michael White and John Gribbin in *Stephen Hawking, A Life in Science.* "His school uniform always looked a mess and, according to his friends, he jabbered rather than talked clearly. . . . He was just that sort of kid—a figure of classroom fun, teased and occasionally bullied, secretly respected by some and avoided by most." He did not look to fulfill the expectations those who had glimpsed his true abilities held for him. The young Stephen, it appears, was the chosen bearer of the frustrated ambitions of his father who was evidently determined that his son would succeed at educational and social goals he, the father, had never quite attained. One goal was to have Stephen attend one of England's most prestigious private schools. . . .

Hawking's personality has been characterized by intense psychological repression. In his family of origin, healthy vulnerability and emotional interaction appear to have been perceived as foreign. At the supper table, the Hawkings would eat without communicating, each head lowered into reading matter. Stephen's childhood home was in a state of physical neglect that went beyond eccentricity to indicate an emotional distance on the part of both parents. . . .

Has it been shown in this chapter that ALS is caused by, or is at least potentiated by, emotional repression? That it is rooted in childhood emotional isolation and loss? That generally—even if not always—it strikes people who lead driven lives and whom others consider to be very "nice"? Until our understanding of the mind/body complex is more advanced, this must remain an intriguing hypothesis but a hypothesis one would be challenged to find any exceptions to. It seems far-fetched to suppose that such frequently observed associations can be all a matter of pure coincidence.

Exercise May Slow the Progression of ALS

Jane Hurly

It has always been thought that exercise makes amyotrophic lateral sclerosis (ALS) worse; however, recent experiments with mice have shown the opposite. Muscles weaken more slowly in mice that exercise than in those that do not, explains Jane Hurly in the following viewpoint. When the fast-twitch muscles used for short bursts of speed are stimulated, she says, they change to slow-twitch muscles, which are less vulnerable to degeneration. Clinical trials with human ALS patients are now being held to find out whether exercise can slow the progression of their disease and improve their quality of life, the author claims.

Hurly is a communications strategist in the Department of Physical Education at the University of Alberta in Canada.

University of Alberta researchers are looking at exercise as a new way to slow the degenerative processes of Amyotrophic Lateral Sclerosis, commonly known as ALS or Lou Gehrig's disease.

Kelvin Jones, a recipient of a 2009 ALS Canada Discovery Grant, has been pioneering research in this field for four years, using mice genetically altered to present familial ALS. He's found that exercise has a positive impact on the mice, slowing the disease significantly.

"Exercise in mice showed a beneficial effect," he said. "We have been looking at the rate of denervation of the muscles [depriving them of a nerve supply] to see how quickly the disease progresses and the muscles weaken. Findings have been very encouraging."

Jones implanted a tiny pacemaker-like device into the transgenic mice, stimulating the fast-twitch muscles, muscles that fatigue easily. These are muscles typically used for short bursts of speed, such as a sprinter would use, but a marathon runner is more likely to have slow-twitch muscles, which are well-vascularized and designed for endurance.

What he found was that by stimulating the fast-twitch muscles (by exercising them repetitively over a long period of time) the fast-twitch muscle changed characteristics, converting to slow-twitch muscle. It was this transformation in the muscles that slowed the progression of ALS in the transgenic mice.

Fast-twitch muscles are more vulnerable to degeneration in ALS patients; therefore, says Jones, "If you have ALS, the more fast-twitch muscle fibre you have, based on the mouse studies, the quicker the symptoms (of ALS) come on.

"What we think is that if we try to build more slow-twitch muscle fibre in ALS patients it would slow the progression of the disease."

FAST FACT

According to the ALS Association, there are people in whom ALS has stopped progressing and a very few in whom the symptoms of ALS have reversed.

Improving Quality of Life

Now Jones is ready to take the next step: to conduct clinical trials with humans. He's optimistic that exercise, which has a proven track record of improving patient survivorship in major diseases, such as cancer and cardiovascular

disease, will show the same benefits in patients with ALS, improving their quality of life, mitigating the impacts of the disease and helping them to survive longer, and with better quality of life.

There have been almost no clinical trials using exercise on people with ALS, says Jones. ALS patients typically participate in drug trials because up to now exercise hasn't usually been offered as a way to mitigate the impacts of the disease. Quite the contrary, he says; neurologists are more likely to prescribe taking it easy because they believe that exercise makes the disease worse and can hasten death—this inactivity causes ALS patients to eventually have more fast-twitch muscles which are vulnerable and degenerate first.

With his new funding Jones will seek opportunities to work with researchers who are conducting drug trials with ALS patients to include an exercise component to their studies, in order to determine what type of exercise prescriptions would be most beneficial.

"Just as physicians want to know with a drug what the dosage should be, how long to take it, and how often,

An ALS sufferer mountain bikes for exercise. Exercise has glowed the progression of the disease in mice, and clinical trials are now being conducted on humans. The results are promising. (© AP Images/Pat Vasquez-Cunningham)

Effect of Exercise on Lifespan in Mice with ALS

Mice with a mutated gene known to cause ALS are used in research. This shows the difference in lifespan between those exposed to no running (red) and early running (blue).

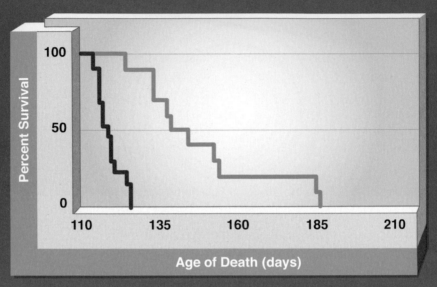

Taken from: Kaspa et al. "Effects of Exercise and Synergy with IGF-1 on Lifespan and Function in ALS Mouse Models," 2005. Springer Images. www.springerimages.com/Images/MedicineAndPublicHealth/1-10.1007_s12017-008-8030-5-0.

so too do they want the same information for an exercise prescription," he says. "Neurologists would love to give advice about physical activity that uses the principles of evidence-based medicine. That's what I want to achieve."

One drug, Riluzone, is the only FDA [Food and Drug Administration]–approved drug for clinical trials. It has been shown to extend life for approximately three months beyond the usual life expectancy of a person with ALS of two to five years.

"It really is about quality of life," says Jones." ALS is incurable, but if exercise can make an ALS patient's life more comfortable, [if] they're better able to manage the disease for longer and it makes their lives a little easier, it's worth pursuing."

Moderate Obesity May Improve Survival in ALS Patients

Amber Dance

Although it is commonly thought that obesity is always bad for health, researchers have found that in the case of people with amyotrophic lateral sclerosis (ALS) this is not true, asserts author Amber Dance in the following viewpoint. Those who are merely overweight live longer than those of normal weight, and those who are moderately—but not extremely—obese live still longer, Dance says, while being underweight hastens death. This may be because heavy people have metabolic reserves to fall back on if the disease causes weight loss, claims the author. A trial is under way to find out whether eating a high-calorie diet will increase ALS patients' survival.

Dance is an award-winning science writer and is the ALS reporter for the Alzheimer Research Forum.

Never mind what you've been hearing about cardiovascular health. Could one life-extending treatment for amyotrophic lateral sclerosis be a bucket of fries and a heaping piece of pie? In the online May [2011] issue of *Muscle & Nerve*, Harvard Medical

SOURCE: Amber Dance, "Being Pleasantly Plump: Way to Live Longest with ALS?" *Alzheimer Research Forum*, May 20, 2011. Available at: http://www.alzforum.org/new/detail.asp?id=2793.

School researchers report that a high body mass index (BMI), indicating mild obesity, was linked to [ALS] survival. Those at the lowest or highest ends of the BMI spectrum fared worst.

This study strongly confirms that increasing BMI seems to represent a valid therapeutic strategy for ALS, wrote Luc Dupuis, of the University of Strasbourg in France, in an e-mail to ARF [Alzheimer Research Forum]. Dupuis was not involved with the study. Senior study author Anne-Marie Wills is pursuing just that strategy in a clinical trial. Wills works at Massachusetts General Hospital in Boston.

In addition to the degeneration of motor neurons and associated symptoms, people with ALS commonly suffer from problems with their metabolism: They eat less, but expend more energy for simple actions such as breathing. Scientists have attempted to correlate the metabolic marker cholesterol and disease prognosis, with conflicting results: One study found that a high ratio of low-density lipoproteins to high-density lipoproteins (LDL/HDL ratio) improved survival, another found no link between LDL/HDL ratio and survival. In contrast, a high HDL/total cholesterol ratio is generally considered good for health.

The Harvard team, led by Wills and first author Sabrina Paganoni of the Spaulding Rehabilitation Hospital in Boston, Massachusetts, addressed the cholesterol question by analyzing data and blood samples from three past studies, and one unpublished study from Massachusetts General Hospital. In all, they correlated cholesterol levels and survival rates from 427 people with ALS. Unlike in some other studies, they carefully adjusted their data for BMI, lung capacity, and age. The result was that lipid levels did not predict survival.

FAST FACT

Among the well-known people who have died from ALS, besides Lou Gehrig, are Chinese leader Mao Tse-tung, US senator Jacob Javits, former US vice president Henry Wallace, heavyweight boxing champ Ezzard Charles, jazz great Charles Mingus, actor David Niven, and singer Dennis Day.

In 2011 Dr. Seward Rutkove won a $1 million prize for developing a reliable way of measuring muscular changes in ALS patients. This will help researchers to test drugs that could slow the progress of the disease. Healthy muscles respond to a painless electrical current differently than deteriorated muscles, which can be seen in these charts of measured voltage.

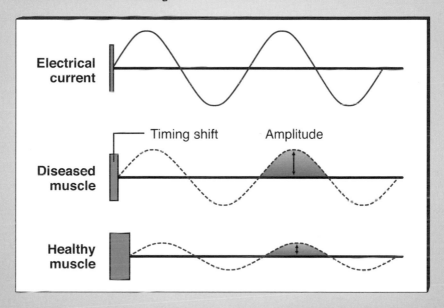

Taken from: Bina Venkataraman. "$1 Million to Inventor of Tracker for A.L.S," *New York Times*, February 3, 2011. www.newyorktimes.com/2011/02/08/health/08/health/08als.html?_r=1&partner=rss&emc=rss.

Heavier Patients Lived Longest

Body mass, however, did. The researchers calculated the percent of mortality within the one- or two-year timeline of each study they used, and found that it produced a U-shaped curve when plotted against BMI. Those who were underweight—with a BMI of less than 18.5—fared the worst, with 44 percent of subjects having passed away by the studies' end. From this low point, survival increased in a stepwise fashion up to a BMI of 30–35, which the

World Health Organization characterizes as the first level of obesity. Only 6 percent of the people in this category died during the studies. From there on outward, survival decreased again, with 52 percent of people whose BMI exceeded 40 passing away.

What made the heavier people live longer? People in the obese category have the buffer of some metabolic reserves, Wills said. Even if they lost weight during the study, at least they had [energy stores] to fall back on. She suspects that the thinner people, in contrast, were forced to break down muscle for energy.

At the high end of the spectrum, Wills hypothesizes that the heaviest people were more likely to suffer cardiovascular disease that contributed to their demise. Dupuis offered another possibility. I would suggest insulin resistance, which, from an energetic point of view, has the same consequences for the cell as starvation (i.e., decreased nutrient entry), he wrote.

Studies have shown that moderately obese ALS patients live longer than underweight patients, which is possibly due to metabolic reserves in the overweight patients. (© pintailpictures/Alamy)

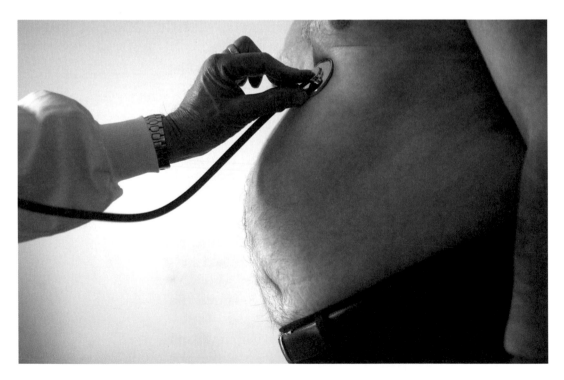

At this point, Wills noted, we cannot say whether this is just an association or whether it is actually causative. But based on these and other data, Wills would want for people with ALS to gain weight, not lose it, in the hopes of slowing progression. She commonly recommends that her patients eat whatever they desire, but finds that many—particularly women resist the idea.

Wills is currently leading a Phase 2 clinical trial of high-fat and high-calorie diets in people with ALS. She is recruiting people who already use feeding tubes in order to precisely control their intake. Although such people are usually far along in their disease course—and thus may not reap much benefit—she hopes with this trial to prove the safety of the overeating approach.

Statin Drugs Do Not Increase the Risk of ALS

Catharine Paddock

According to Catharine Paddock in the following viewpoint, an analysis by the Food and Drug Administration (FDA) has not shown any link between statins—which are drugs used to lower cholesterol—and an increased risk of amyotrophic lateral sclerosis (ALS). The FDA performed this analysis through a technique known as data mining, in which data about a specific topic is extracted from information sources that were originally produced for other reasons. In this case it asked drug companies that make statins to report how many ALS cases were diagnosed during their drug trials, says Paddock. It looked at the results of forty-one trials and did not find any more ALS in subjects who took statins than in those given placebos, says the author, despite the fact that there have been an unexpectedly large number of ALS cases reported in people who have taken statins since the trials. The FDA has stated that further study is warranted, says Paddock, but in the meantime its official position is that there need be no reduction in the use of statins.

Paddock is a writer and independent consultant.

SOURCE: Catharine Paddock, "Statins Not Linked to Higher Risk of ALS, Says FDA," *Medical News Today,* September 30, 2008. Copyright © 2008 by Medical News Today All rights reserved. Reproduced by permission.

A new analysis by the US Food and Drug Administration (FDA) of data from over 40 clinical trials did not show a link between statins, drugs used to lower cholesterol, and higher risk of amyotrophic lateral sclerosis (ALS), a neurodegenerative disease often referred to as "Lou Gehrig's Disease". The FDA said there is no need to change prescribing practice. The analysis is reported as a study in the 29 September [2008] issue of *Pharmacoepidemiology and Drug Safety* by FDA researchers.

ALS is a fatal neurodegenerative condition that affects about 1 to 2 per 100,000 people. Its incidence increases with age. ALS is a type of motor neuron disease where brain cells that control muscle movement gradually stop working and the person eventually loses the ability to move any part of the body apart from the eyes.

The FDA study is an example of the increasing use of an investigative method called data mining. Traditionally a tool of corporate knowledge management specialists,

The US Food and Drug Administration reviewed the data from forty-one placebo-controlled statin trials and found nine cases of ALS in statin-treated patients and ten cases in those treated with placebo. (© Cordelia Molloy/Photo Researchers, Inc.)

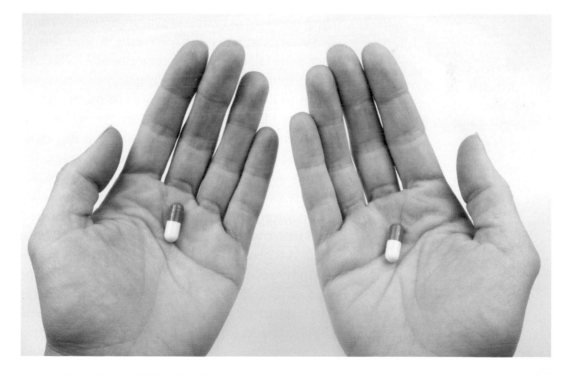

data mining is a systematic way of extracting data relevant to a specific topic or question from a collection of information sources originally produced for other reasons. Researchers are increasingly using this discipline to mine studies with a common theme to look for coherent patterns that suggest other things could also be happening in the data set.

The FDA wondered if such a pattern might be that statin use was in some way linked to an increased incidence of ALS because they were getting a higher than expected number of Adverse Event Reporting System (AERS) reports of ALS in patients on statins. They received 91 such reports in all, some from inside and some from outside the US.

Analyzing the Data

First, two FDA neurologists individually reviewed all AERS cases of ALS reported in association with the use of a statin. Then they asked drug companies making the statins lovastatin, pravastatin, simvastatin, fluvastatin, atorvastatin, cerivastatin, and rosuvastatin to tell them how many cases of ALS were diagnosed during all of their placebo-controlled statin trials that lasted 6 months or more.

The FDA investigators then reviewed the data from 41 placebo-controlled statin trials that lasted between 6 months and 5 years, totalling around 200,000 patient-years of exposure to a statin and about the same to a placebo. They found that 9 cases of ALS were reported in statin-treated patients and 10 cases in those treated with placebo. They concluded that: "Although we observed a data mining signal for ALS with statins in FDA's AERS, retrospective analyses of 41 statin clinical trials did not reveal an increased incidence of ALS in subjects treated with a statin compared with placebo."

> **FAST FACT**
>
> There are three small regions in the western Pacific where ALS has been more common than elsewhere in the world—the area of Guam inhabited by the Chamorro people, West Papua, and the Kii Peninsula of Japan.

Incidence of ALS per 100,000 People Age 45–74

Country/Region	Male	Female	Overall
United States (WA)	5.3	4.9	5.1
United States (MN)	7.1	6.0	6.6
United States (TX)	3.4	3.2	3.3
Canada	6.7	4.2	5.3
Japan	3.4	3.2	3.3
Greece	3.1	1.8	2.4
Denmark	5.0	3.6	4.2
Finland	7.4	8.9	8.2

Taken from: S. Cronin, O. Hardiman, and B.J. Traynor. "Ethnic Variation in the Incidence of ALS—A Systematic Review," *Neurology* 68, 2007, pp. 1,002–1,007.

One of the investigators, Dr. Mark Avigan, director of the Division of Pharmacovigilance I, at the FDA's Center for Drug Evaluation and Research, said:

> While the FDA finds the lack of an increase in the incidence of amyotrophic lateral sclerosis (ALS) in patients treated with statins in clinical trials reassuring, given the extensive use of this class of drugs and the serious nature of ALS, continued study of this issue is warranted.

The FDA is waiting for the completion of a large study of ALS and statin use by Dr. Lorene Nelson, Chief of the Division of Epidemiology at Stanford University School of Medicine, and colleagues from the Division of Research at Kaiser Permanente, which should finish in 6 to 9 months [in 2009], and the agency is also considering carrying out further epidemiologic studies of its own.

Statins, or HMG-CoA-reductase inhibitors, are the most commonly-prescribed drug for reducing elevated cholesterol levels in the US.

CHAPTER 3

Personal Narratives

A World-Famous Scientist Tells About His Life with ALS

Stephen Hawking

British physicist and cosmologist Stephen Hawking is one of the most prominent scientists in the world and has received many scientific honors. In addition, he has written best-selling books for the public as well as numerous scientific papers. Yet he has had amyotrophic lateral sclerosis (ALS) for nearly fifty years, far longer than its victims usually survive. In the following article he tells about how it first struck him when he was twenty-one and how he adjusted to living with it. Because Hawking's work was considered important, he was one of the first people to receive a computer and speech synthesizer to enable him to communicate. Besides teaching at Cambridge University, he has given many lectures and has appeared on various television shows, including *Star Trek*. Despite being almost totally paralyzed, Hawking lives as normal a life as possible and considers himself lucky because of the help he has received from family, friends, and organizations.

Photo on facing page. An ALS sufferer uses a special stand to line up and roll her bowling ball. Many ALS patients adapt to their illness and lead relatively happy lives. (© AP Images/Peter Bauer)

I am quite often asked: How do you feel about having ALS? The answer is, not a lot. I try to lead as normal a life as possible, and not think about my condition, or regret the things it prevents me from doing, which are not that many.

It was a great shock to me to discover that I had motor neurone disease. I had never been very well co-ordinated physically as a child. I was not good at ball games, and my handwriting was the despair of my teachers. Maybe for this reason, I didn't care much for sport or physical activities. But things seemed to change when I went to Oxford, at the age of 17. I took up coxing [directing the rowers] and rowing. I was not Boat Race standard, but I got by at the level of inter-College competition.

In my third year at Oxford, however, I noticed that I seemed to be getting more clumsy, and I fell over once or twice for no apparent reason. But it was not until I was at Cambridge, in the following year, that my father noticed, and took me to the family doctor. He referred me to a specialist, and shortly after my 21st birthday, I went into hospital for tests. I was in for two weeks, during which I had a wide variety of tests. They took a muscle sample from my arm, stuck electrodes into me, and injected some radio opaque fluid into my spine, and watched it going up and down with x-rays, as they tilted the bed. After all that, they didn't tell me what I had, except that it was not multiple sclerosis, and that I was an a-typical case. I gathered, however, that they expected it to continue to get worse, and that there was nothing they could do, except give me vitamins. I could see that they didn't expect them to have much effect. I didn't feel like asking for more details, because they were obviously bad.

FAST FACT

ALS is called Lou Gehrig's disease only in the United States and Canada; in Britain and elsewhere it is called motor neurone—or motor neuron—disease (MND). In France it is sometimes called Charcot's disease, after the French neurologist who first recognized it.

A Shocking Realisation

The realisation that I had an incurable disease, that was likely to kill me in a few years, was a bit of a shock. How could something like that happen to me? Why should I be cut off like this? However, while I had been in hospital, I had seen a boy I vaguely knew die of leukaemia, in the bed opposite me. It had not been a pretty sight. Clearly there were people who were worse off than me. At least my condition didn't make me feel sick. Whenever I feel inclined to be sorry for myself I remember that boy.

Not knowing what was going to happen to me, or how rapidly the disease would progress, I was at a loose end. The doctors told me to go back to Cambridge and carry on with the research I had just started in general relativity and cosmology. But I was not making much progress, because I didn't have much mathematical background. And, anyway, I might not live long enough to finish my PhD. I felt somewhat of a tragic character. I took to listening to [German composer of dramatic operas Richard] Wagner, but reports in magazine articles that I drank heavily are an exaggeration. The trouble is once one article said it, other articles copied it, because it made a good story. People believe that anything that has appeared in print so many times must be true.

Something to Live For

My dreams at that time were rather disturbed. Before my condition had been diagnosed, I had been very bored with life. There had not seemed to be anything worth doing. But shortly after I came out of hospital, I dreamt that I was going to be executed. I suddenly realised that there were a lot of worthwhile things I could do if I were reprieved. Another dream, that I had several times, was that I would sacrifice my life to save others. After all, if I were going to die anyway, it might as well do some good. But I didn't die. In fact, although there was a cloud hanging over my future, I found, to my surprise, that I was enjoying life in the present more than before. I began to make progress with my research, and I got engaged to a girl called Jane Wilde, whom I had met just about the time my condition was diagnosed. That engagement changed my life. It gave me something to live for. But it also meant that I had to get a job if we were to get married. I therefore applied for a research fellowship at Gonville and Caius (pronounced Keys) college, Cambridge. To my great surprise, I got a fellowship, and we got married a few months later.

The fellowship at Caius took care of my immediate employment problem. I was lucky to have chosen to work in theoretical physics, because that was one of the few areas in which my condition would not be a serious handicap. And I was fortunate that my scientific reputation increased, at the same time that my disability got worse. This meant that people were prepared to offer me a sequence of positions in which I only had to do research, without having to lecture.

Finding Suitable Housing

We were also fortunate in housing. When we were married, Jane was still an undergraduate at Westfield College in London, so she had to go up to London during the week. This meant that we had to find somewhere I could manage on my own, and which was central, because I could not walk far. I asked the College if they could help, but was told by the then Bursar [financial administrator for a university]: it is College policy not to help Fellows with housing. We therefore put our name down to rent one of a group of new flats that were being built in the market place. (Years later, I discovered that those flats were actually owned by the College, but they didn't tell me that.) However, when we returned to Cambridge from a visit to America after the marriage, we found that the flats were not ready. As a great concession, the Bursar said we could have a room in a hostel for graduate students. He said, "We normally charge 12 shillings and 6 pence a night for this room. However, as there will be two of you in the room, we will charge 25 shillings." We stayed there only three nights. Then we found a small house about 100 yards from my university department. It belonged to another College, who had let it to one of its fellows. However he had moved out to a house he had bought in the suburbs. He sub-let the house to us for the remaining three months of his lease. During those three months, we found that another house in the same road was standing empty. A neighbour summoned the owner from Dorset, and told her that it was a scandal that her house should be empty, when young people were looking for accommodation. So she let the house to us. After we had lived there for a few years, we wanted to buy the house, and do it up. So we asked my College for a mortgage. However, the College did a survey, and decided it was not a good risk. In the end we got a mortgage from a building society, and my parents gave us the money to do it up. We lived there for another four years, but it became too difficult for me to manage the stairs. By this time, the College appreciated me rather more, and there was a different Bursar. They therefore offered us a ground floor flat in a house that they owned. This suited me very well, because it had large rooms and wide doors. It was sufficiently central that I could get to my University department, or the College, in my electric wheel chair. It was also nice for our three children, because it was surrounded by garden, which was looked after by the College gardeners.

Help with Speaking and Writing

Up to 1974, I was able to feed myself, and get in and out of bed. Jane managed to help me, and bring up the children, without outside help. However, things were getting more difficult, so we took to having one of my research students living with us. In return for free accommodation, and a lot of my attention, they helped me get up and go to bed. In 1980, we changed to a system of community and private nurses, who came in for an hour or two in the morning and evening. This lasted until I caught pneumonia in 1985. I had to have a tracheotomy operation [a breathing tube inserted into the windpipe through a slit in the throat]. After this, I had to have 24 hour nursing care. This was made possible by grants from several foundations.

Before the operation, my speech had been getting more slurred, so that only a few people who knew me well, could understand me. But at least I could communicate. I wrote scientific papers by dictating to a secretary, and I gave seminars through an interpreter, who repeated my words more clearly. However, the tracheotomy operation removed my ability to speak altogether. For a time, the only way I could communicate was to spell out words letter by letter, by raising my eyebrows when someone pointed to the right letter on a spelling card. It is pretty difficult to carry on a conversation like that, let alone write a scientific paper. However, a computer expert in California, called Walt Woltosz, heard of my plight. He sent me a computer program he had written, called Equalizer. This allowed me to select words from a series of menus on the screen, by pressing a switch in my hand. The program could also be controlled by a switch, operated by head or eye movement. When I have built up what I want to say, I can send it to a speech synthesizer. At first, I just ran the Equalizer program on a desk top computer.

Synthesised Speech—with an American Accent

However David Mason, of Cambridge Adaptive Communication, fitted a small portable computer and a speech synthesizer to my wheel chair. This system allowed me to communicate much better than I could before. I can manage up to 15 words a minute. I can either speak what I have written, or save it to disk. I can then print it out, or call it back and speak it sentence by sentence. Using this system, I have written a book, and dozens of scientific papers. I have also given many scientific and popular talks. They have all been well received. I think that is in a large part due to the quality of the speech synthesiser, which is made by Speech Plus. One's voice is very important. If you have a slurred voice, people are likely to treat you as mentally deficient: Does he take sugar? This synthesiser is by far the best I have heard, because it varies the intonation, and doesn't speak like a Dalek [a fictional alien race on the British TV series *Dr. Who*]. The only trouble is that it gives me an American accent.

No Need to Lose Hope

I have had motor neurone disease for practically all my adult life. Yet it has not prevented me from having a very attractive family, and being successful in my work. This is thanks to the help I have received from Jane, my children, and a large number of other people and organisations. I have been lucky, that my condition has progressed more slowly than is often the case. But it shows that one need not lose hope.

Teenage Couple Faces a Deadly Diagnosis

Allen G. Breed

Sabrina Parker was an average teenager who enjoyed Facebook, the *Twilight* movies, and sports and who had a devoted boyfriend, Matt Scozzari, says Allen G. Breed in the following article. But Sabrina's mother and grandmother had both died of amyotrophic lateral sclerosis (ALS), and when she was only fifteen she began having symptoms of it, too. After doctors confirmed that she had the inherited form of ALS, reports Breed, she could not bring herself to tell Matt, but on the night of her sixteenth birthday party some of her friends told him. Matt vowed that he would support her and would never leave her, although his parents worried about his being in love with a terminally ill girl. Sabrina's disease progressed rapidly; she had to have a feeding tube and later tried a ventilator, which she found too uncomfortable. She and Matt wanted to be married, the author says, but since that was impractical, they had a friendship ceremony that was similar to a wedding. Not long afterward, Sabrina died in her sleep, while Matt sat beside her, holding her hand.

Breed is a writer for the Associated Press, an international news service.

As she walked through the door, Sabrina Parker's big hazel eyes flared with surprise and she raised a hand to her mouth to stifle a gasp. She was a huge fan of the "Twilight" book and movie series, and her friends and family had transformed this greasy garage into a Sweet 16's dream.

Homemade strobe lights illuminated walls decorated like the night sky and plastered with cast posters. All around were balloons in red, white and black. An enormous cake, iced to look like the chess board on one of the book jackets, held 16 blazing candles.

The crowd began chanting for Sabrina to blow them out. She bent in close and blew, but the flames barely flickered. She straightened up and shook her head. Realizing her distress, Matt Scozzari stepped closer and told her they would do it together. On the count of three, they leaned in and snuffed them out together.

In the three months since he'd first asked her out, Matt had noticed small changes in his girlfriend: The shortness of breath, the slurring in her speech, the weight loss. When he'd ask what was going on, Sabrina would just shrug it off as nothing serious.

But Sabrina knew her condition was very serious. About a month after she started seeing Matt, Sabrina learned that she had amyotrophic lateral sclerosis [ALS], also known as Lou Gehrig's Disease—the same illness that had killed her mother and grandmother. A doctor told Sabrina it wouldn't be long before she would have to decide whether to go on a ventilator. She'd told her closest friends about her condition, but she hadn't been able to bring herself to tell Matt.

Matt had been so sweet and gentle. For her Sweet 16, he'd bought matching pewter replicas of Bella's and Edward's rings from *Twilight: New Moon*, inscribed with the words, "What would I do without you?" How would he react when he found out she had this horrible, wasting disease—that she was dying? She was petrified. She had already lost so much, and would lose so much more in the coming months. She didn't want to risk losing Matt, too.

In Sabrina's favorite song, there's a refrain that goes: "Time slows down/Whenever you're around/Can you feel/This magic in the air?" The song, by Taylor Swift, is called "Today Was a Fairy Tale." Sabrina and Matt would understand soon enough that their story could have no happily-ever-after ending. The "magic" would be in how the brave and devoted ninth graders chose to use the time they had.

In so many ways, Sabrina Kay Parker was an average teenage girl. She was all about Facebook and Aeropostale. She played volleyball and softball. She loved roller skating and roller coasters, Taco Bell and *Twilight* hunk Taylor Lautner. But a genetic abnormality made her unlike almost anyone else. Her maternal grandmother, Lorna Kay Melton, died of ALS on Feb. 2, 1993, a year before her granddaughter's birth. Sabrina was around 3 when her mother, Melissa Kay Melton, began showing symptoms and just 4 years old when "Missy" died. Sabrina's father, Asheston Parker, soon remarried, and the redheaded 6-year-old went to live with his parents, Noland and Zelma Parker. The Parkers lived in constant dread that Sabrina would fall ill. Lorna had been 46 when she died; Missy had been 24. Sensing a pattern, Noland wouldn't breathe easy until Sabrina celebrated her 12th birthday without symptoms. When she passed that milestone, and then her 13th and 14th, he dared to hope that the girl he and his wife had come to consider their own daughter had broken the family curse. But in June 2009, Sabrina began complaining of earaches. Her voice had begun to grow more nasal and difficult to understand. Her grandparents took her to an ear, nose and throat specialist, but he could find no abnormalities.

Not long after she began eighth grade that fall, Sabrina asked her grandparents to write a note to her gym teacher, excusing her from doing sit-ups: She couldn't lift her head off the floor without putting her hand behind her neck. . . .

The next time they took her to the doctor about her ears, the grandparents mentioned Sabrina's sad family history. A pediatric neurologist ordered CT [computerized tomography] scans, an MRI [magnetic resonance imaging scan], electromyography to evaluate the electrical activity produced by skeletal muscles. Sabrina even spent a night in a sleep lab.

"i didnt really sleep that good because i had all theas wires attached to me," she posted on Facebook.

Perhaps there was another reason: The test began on Nov. 6, 2009, the day Matt Scozzari finally worked up the nerve to ask her out. . . .

Matt was more than a year younger than Sabrina, who had repeated a grade. There was something about Sabrina—a feistiness, a spark in her eye—that reminded him of his grandmother. After admiring her from afar for months, Matt approached her in gym class and asked her out. She said yes without hesitating. They went to movies and the mall. Matt waited a month before kissing her for the first time.

Sabrina did her best to hide her illness, but it was getting harder every day. Her speech was becoming more difficult to understand, and she was having trouble with drooling. Besides, she really didn't have anything to tell Matt. All the tests—including a blood scan for the SOD1 gene, a common marker for familial ALS—had come back normal.

But her doctor, fearing this was ALS, referred the family to one of the leaders in the field: Dr. Richard Bedlack, director of the Duke Health Center's neuroscience clinic. Last December [2009], the family made the three-hour trip to Durham.

The girl Bedlack examined could speak fairly clearly, but her tongue movement was weak. Her arms showed signs of atrophy, the left worse than the right. Her "forced vital capacity"—the amount of air she could blow into a tube—was 89 percent of normal. She weighed just 105 pounds, about 32 pounds below normal for her 5-foot-6 frame.

ALS is hereditary in only 10 percent of cases. Bedlack would need to do some genetic testing to confirm it, but he was already certain of his diagnosis. Sabrina was too young to remember her mother's battle with the disease, but she had been reading up on ALS. Hearing Bedlack say the words aloud, she wept.

Normally, the younger the patient, the slower the disease's progression. But Sabrina was deteriorating rapidly. When the girl had calmed down, Bedlack told her and the Parkers that they had a lot of decisions to make during the next six months about how aggressive they wanted to be. Would she want a tracheostomy [permanent breathing tube in her throat]? A ventilator? He suggested Sabrina draft a living will to make her wishes clear. For now, she agreed to have a feeding tube inserted. The surgery was done three days later.

> ## FAST FACT
>
> It is extremely rare for ALS to appear in teens. When it happens it is usually the inherited form of the disease and relatives are known to have had it.

The tube was just to help her get her weight back up, Sabrina assured Matt, but his mother wasn't buying it. "Everything you're telling me sounds like something very serious," Audrey Scozzari told her son. "You need to be prepared for this."

Sabrina's 16th birthday was on Feb. 6. On Facebook, she gushed about the green satin dress she'd picked out for the occasion; Matt escorted her to the party. After Sabrina had opened her gifts, two of her friends asked Matt to step outside. He could see they were on the verge of tears. "Matt, it's about Sabrina," one said. "She's got Lou Gehrig's disease." Matt didn't exactly know what that was, but he knew it was bad. His head swimming, he made his way to the pond on the property, sat down and began to weep. Sabrina found Matt there. "Are you going to leave me now?" she asked. "I will never leave you," he replied. "No matter what." They held each other and cried.

Later, Matt shared the news with his mother. Audrey Scozzari was a hospice volunteer and had cared for her mother in her final seven months. She explained the course that Sabrina's illness was likely to take.

"Matthew, that's a lot for you to take on, son," she said.

"Mom," he replied through his tears. "I can't just walk out on her."

Sabrina was facing some tough decisions, she told him, and it would be his job to support her. "This is her journey," she said. "You can walk beside her, but you cannot control her journey for her." . . .

When the doctor told [Sabrina] it was about time to make a decision about a ventilator, she turned to Matt and asked him what she should do. "If it were up to me, I would want you to get it," he told her. "We'll be able to spend more time together."

Again, she put it off. But her journal reveals she was wrestling with whether to artificially prolong her life. "i dont want to miss the prom," she wrote, "i want to be able to finsh high school and go to collage get a job get married and have kids of my own but i dnt like the way thing are going but its life and sometimes i think to myslef why dose it have to be me"

Sabrina began her freshman year at White Oak High School in late August. By the end of the first week, she had already logged her first sick day. Barely three weeks into the school year, she decided to get the tracheostomy.

"kinda scared," she wrote on Facebook. "after the surgery have to stay 2 weeks in the hospital."

Surgeons placed the trach tube on Sept. 23. She agreed to try a ventilator, but quickly decided it was too painful and uncomfortable. On Oct. 6, she went home. . . .

The Scozzaris could tell that their 15-year-old son was madly in love with this terminally ill girl. And it worried them. Matt began starting sentences with, "When Sabrina and I get married. . . . " Sabrina had taken to calling herself Sabrina Kay Scozzari, even sometimes signing her notes that way. Finally, Audrey Scozzari sat her son down and explained that marriage, though not impossible, was impractical. Then she suggested an alternative.

"You know, they have something called a friendship ceremony," she told Matt. "That could be your way of letting her experience what a wedding would be like." . . .

Sabrina had asked her grandparents to buy her a wedding dress for the occasion, but they thought that inappropriate. She settled for a lovely ivory sheath embroidered with gold, with a matching gold shawl. One of Sabrina's nurses did her hair in a double row of French braids.

Matt met Sabrina at the car and escorted her inside the same garage where homecoming had been held. This time, the rafters were strung with Christmas lights, and the cold concrete floor was strewn with red, pink and white rose petals. The couple sat holding hands as the minister led prayers. Twice, Sabrina had to be suctioned [to clear her trach tube].

When the time came for the vows, the crowd came closer, forming a circle around the couple. Matt turned to Sabrina and clasped her hands in his. "Sabrina. I know that these few months or the year that we've been dating have been really hard," he said in a halting but firm voice. "We've had our ups and downs, but I KNOW that whatever happens, that I know I want to stay with you—and that I wish it would be longer."

He had changed, he said, "from somebody who didn't really care to somebody who had something to live for and care for," he said. "Being around you just makes me smile . . . I'm hoping that you think the same way."

Sabrina smiled and nodded.

Matt had placed two small boxes on the petal-strewn table. He opened them to reveal matching silver bands—[traditional Irish] Claddagh rings, with a pair of hands clutching a heart topped by a crown. "It was hard to find your size," he said, slipping the ring on the third finger of her right hand. "But I hope it's close enough."

Sabrina reached for the other ring, but her fingers were trembling and weak. Matt gently took hold of her hand and helped her guide the band over his knuckle.

All around them, there was applause, and tears. . . .

Later, back home and unable to sleep, Sabrina logged onto Facebook. "tonight was the most amazing night ever," she wrote, "iam glad that me and matt got t odo the freindship ceremonoy together i love what matt said and he is the love of my life matthew i love you i will be with you no matter what happens"

A couple of hours later, Matt posted his own message: "Tonight you made me feel like the luckiest man alive!!"

Diagnosed with ALS at fifteen, Sabrina Parker is pictured with her boyfriend Matt Scozzari at their friendship ceremony on November 20, 2010. She would pass away in her sleep ten days later, at age sixteen. (© AP Images/Gerry Broome) he wrote. "i hope tonight proved that I would walk to the ends of the earth and back for you. I may not be able to offer you diamonds and everything your heart desires but I hope that my love for you will be enough at the moment. No matter what the future has in store for you (us) know that I will be there with you forever and always!!"

On Thanksgiving Day, Sabrina's condition deteriorated rapidly. By Saturday, she could no longer raise her head.

Around midnight on Nov. 29, the Parkers called Matt: He'd better come. He stayed with Sabrina through the night, holding her hand and telling her he would be OK. Sabrina died in her sleep the next morning. When the hearse came, Matt leaned down to kiss her on the forehead. . . .

She was buried in her Sweet 16 dress, a single red rose from Matt on the pillow beside her head.

"Night," from *The Memory Chalet*

Tony Judt

In the following article writer Tony Judt tells how difficult it is to live with the paralysis caused by amyotrophic lateral sclerosis (ALS), especially during the night when his nurse is sleeping. At first it was all he could do not to call out for help; later he learned to focus on his own thoughts, memories, and fantasies. While the thought that he will have to go through this helplessness and isolation night after night for the rest of his life is intolerable, he is able to manage one night at a time.

Judt, a British historian, essayist, and university professor, died in 2010. He authored many books about European history.

I suffer from a motor neuron disorder, in my case a variant of amyotrophic lateral schlerosis (ALS): Lou Gehrig's disease. Motor neuron disorders are far from rare: Parkinson's disease, multiple sclerosis, and a variety of lesser diseases all come under that heading. What is distinctive about ALS—the least common of this family of neuro-muscular illnesses—is firstly that there is no loss of sensation (a mixed blessing) and secondly that there is no pain. In contrast to almost every other serious or deadly disease, one is thus left free to contemplate at leisure and in minimal discomfort the catastrophic progress of one's own deterioration.

In effect, ALS constitutes progressive imprisonment without parole. First you lose the use of a digit or two; then a limb; then and almost inevitably, all four. The muscles of the torso decline into near torpor, a practical problem from the digestive point of view but also life-threatening, in that breathing becomes at first difficult and eventually impossible without external assistance in the form of a tube-and-pump apparatus. In the more extreme variants of the disease, associated with dysfunction of the upper motor neurons (the rest of the body is driven by the so-called lower motor neurons), swallowing, speaking, and even controlling the jaw and head become impossible. I do not (yet) suffer from this aspect of the disease, or else I could not dictate this text.

By my present stage of decline, I am thus effectively quadriplegic. With extraordinary effort I can move my right hand a little and can adduct my left arm some six inches across my chest. My legs, although they will lock when upright long enough to allow a nurse to transfer me from one chair to another, cannot bear my weight and only one of them has any autonomous movement left in it. Thus when legs or arms are set in a given position, there they remain until someone moves them for me. The same is true of my torso, with the result that backache from inertia and pressure is a chronic irritation. Having no use of my arms, I cannot scratch an itch, adjust my spectacles, remove food particles from my teeth, or anything else that—as a moment's reflection will confirm—we all do dozens of times a day. To say the least, I am utterly and completely dependent upon the kindness of strangers (and anyone else).

During the day I can at least request a scratch, an adjustment, a drink, or simply a gratuitous re-placement of my limbs—since enforced stillness for hours on end is not only physically uncomfortable but psychologically close to intolerable. It is not as though you lose the desire to stretch, to bend, to stand or lie or run or even exercise. But when the urge comes over you there is nothing—nothing—that you can do except seek some tiny substitute or else find a way to suppress the thought and the accompanying muscle memory.

But then comes the night. I leave bedtime until the last possible moment compatible with my nurse's need for sleep. Once I have been "prepared" for bed I am rolled into the bedroom in the wheelchair where I have spent the past eighteen hours. With some difficulty (despite my reduced height, mass, and bulk I am still a substantial dead weight for even a strong man to shift) I am maneuvered onto my cot. I am sat upright at an angle of some 110° and wedged into place with folded towels and pillows, my left leg in particular turned out ballet-like to compensate for its propensity to collapse inward. This process requires considerable concentration. If I allow a stray limb to be mis-placed, or fail to insist on having my midriff carefully aligned with legs and head, I shall suffer the agonies of the damned later in the night.

> **FAST FACT**
>
> Although scientists used to believe that ALS does not affect the mind, new research has shown that some ALS patients do experience mild or moderate forms of cognitive impairment.

I am then covered, my hands placed outside the blanket to afford me the illusion of mobility but wrapped nonetheless since—like the rest of me—they now suffer from a permanent sensation of cold. I am offered a final scratch on any of a dozen itchy spots from hairline to toe; the Bi-Pap breathing device in my nose is adjusted to a necessarily uncomfortable level of tightness to ensure that it does not slip in the night; my glasses are removed . . . and there I lie: trussed, myopic, and motionless like a modern-day mummy, alone in my corporeal prison, accompanied for the rest of the night only by my thoughts.

Of course, I do have access to help if I need it. Since I can't move a muscle, save only my neck and head, my communication device is a baby's intercom at my bedside, left permanently on so that a mere call from me will bring assistance. In the early stages of my disease the temptation to call out for help was almost irresistible: every muscle felt in need of movement, every inch of skin itched, my bladder found mysterious ways to refill itself in the night and thus require relief, and in general I felt a desperate need for the reassurance of light, company, and the simple comforts of human intercourse. By now, however, I have learned to forgo this most nights, finding solace and recourse in my own thoughts.

The latter, though I say it myself, is no small undertaking. Ask yourself how often you move in the night. I don't mean change location altogether (e.g., to go to the bathroom, though that too): merely how often you shift a hand, a foot; how frequently you scratch assorted body parts before dropping off; how unselfconsciously you alter position very slightly to find the most comfortable one. Imagine for a moment that you had been obliged instead to lie absolutely motionless on your back—by no means the best sleeping position, but the only one I can tolerate—for seven unbroken hours and constrained to come up with ways to render this Calvary tolerable not just for one night but for the rest of your life.

My solution has been to scroll through my life, my thoughts, my fantasies, my memories, mis-memories, and the like until I have chanced upon events, people, or narratives that I can employ to divert my mind from the body in which it is encased. These mental exercises have to be interesting enough to hold my attention and see me through an intolerable itch in my inner ear or lower back; but they also have to be boring and predictable enough to serve as a reliable prelude and encouragement to sleep. It took me some time to identify this process as a workable alternative to insomnia and physical discomfort and it is by no means infallible. But I am occasionally astonished, when I reflect upon the matter, at how readily I seem to get through, night after night, week after week, month after month, what was once an almost insufferable nocturnal ordeal. I wake up in exactly the position, frame of mind, and state of suspended despair with which I went to bed—which in the circumstances might be thought a considerable achievement.

This cockroach-like existence is cumulatively intolerable even though on any given night it is perfectly manageable. "Cockroach" is of course an allusion to [surrealist author Franz] Kafka's *Metamorphosis*, in which the protagonist wakes up one morning to discover that he has been transformed into an insect. The point of the story is as much the responses and incomprehension of his family as it is the account of his own sensations, and it is hard to resist the thought that even the best-meaning and most generously thoughtful friend or relative cannot hope to understand the sense of isolation and imprisonment that this disease imposes upon its victims. Helplessness is humiliating even in a passing crisis—imagine or recall some occasion when you have fallen down or otherwise required physical assistance from strangers. Imagine the mind's response to the knowledge that the peculiarly humiliating helplessness of ALS is a life sentence (we speak blithely of death sentences in this connection, but actually the latter would be a relief).

Morning brings some respite, though it says something about the lonely journey through the night that the prospect of being transferred to a wheelchair for the rest of the day should raise one's spirits! Having something to do, in my case something purely cerebral and verbal, is a salutary diversion—if only in the almost literal sense of providing an occasion to communicate with the outside world and express in words, often angry words, the bottled-up irritations and frustrations of physical inanition.

The best way to survive the night would be to treat it like the day. If I could find people who had nothing better to do than talk to me all night about something sufficiently diverting to keep us both awake, I would search them out. But one is also and always aware in this disease of the necessary *normalcy* of other people's lives: their need for exercise, entertainment, and sleep. And so my nights superficially resemble those of other people. I prepare for bed; I go to bed; I get up (or, rather, am got up). But the bit between is, like the disease itself, incommunicable.

I suppose I should be at least mildly satisfied to know that I have found within myself the sort of survival mechanism that most normal people only read about in accounts of natural disasters or isolation cells. And it is true that this disease has its enabling dimension: thanks to my inability to take notes or prepare them, my memory—already quite good—has improved considerably, with the help of techniques adapted from the "memory palace" so intriguingly depicted by [historian] Jonathan Spence. But the satisfactions of compensation are notoriously fleeting. There is no saving grace in being confined to an iron suit, cold and unforgiving. The pleasures of mental agility are much overstated, inevitably—as it now appears to me—by those not exclusively dependent upon them. Much the same can be said of well-meaning encouragements to find nonphysical compensations for physical inadequacy. That way lies futility. Loss is loss, and nothing is gained by calling it by a nicer name. My nights are intriguing; but I could do without them.

A Woman with ALS Makes a Controversial TV Public Service Ad

Sarah Ezekiel

A television ad aimed at raising public awareness of amyotrophic lateral sclerosis (ALS) was filmed for British television in 2008, but it was banned by a watchdog organization that considered it too shocking, leading to a heated controversy in the media. In the following blog entry, Sarah Ezekiel, an ALS patient who appeared in the ad, tells how it was filmed and expresses her disappointment about the ban. She believes that many shocking things are shown on TV and that viewers should be told about the terrible effects of a real disease from which people are suffering, which only a graphic presentation can convey.

Ezekiel is a single parent who was stricken by ALS when she was thirty-four.

E verything was pretty straightforward for me until the age of 34. I was happily married with a beautiful little girl and pregnant with my much longed for second child. In February 2000, I noticed

SOURCE: Sarah Ezekiel, "Guest Writer Sarah Ezekiel Blogs on 'Sarah's Story' Controversy," Prize4Life, August 11, 2009. blog.prize 4life.org.

some weakness in my left arm and my speech was slurring. By April 2000, I had a definite diagnosis of ALS or Motor Neurone Disease (MND) as it's called in the UK.

It happened so quickly; I was absolutely terrified. My marriage collapsed as I became progressively disabled. I couldn't physically care for my children or myself anymore, and spiraled into deep depression. I'm now a single, disabled parent who is totally dependent on caregivers for everything. I never expected my life to change so tragically. I often think that it's more painful for my family and friends than it is for me.

I am now 43 and have survived much longer than most ALS sufferers. I have lost almost all my mobility, as well as my speech. I use a program called E Z Keys on my laptop, which enables me to communicate and access the internet. Technology has saved me!

When I was asked to appear in "Sarah's Story", the ALS advertisement that has been the subject of so much controversy, I didn't hesitate. Donna Cresswell from the MND Association showed me the story boards and explained more about the film. I liked the concept and felt that it was important for the public to see.

Making a Video for TV

On the 3rd of July 2008, I found myself in a studio in Central London. My first scene was the end one, sitting in the huge wheelchair. I was positioned and had to keep very still, and when that finished, I was told that was it.

I asked whether I had just come there to sit in a wheelchair, feeling pretty upset. I asked the director whether I could try some other scenes because I wanted to show the deterioration that ALS causes to the body. I kept insisting until he agreed. I went home feeling pleased and amazed by the dedication and kindness of the creatives, director, actress and the crew, who gave their time for free.

FAST FACT

Ride for Life, a nonprofit organization founded to raise public awareness about and research funding for ALS, holds an annual event in which ALS patients ride their electric wheelchairs from New York's Yankee Stadium to Washington, DC, and from Montauk Point (the tip of Long Island, New York) to Manhattan.

The advertisement that we worked so hard on was recently banned from television by the British watchdog, Clearcast. They told us that it was "too shocking" for people to see.

I was, and remain, very disappointed with this decision. There are many shocking adverts [advertisements] being shown on British TV, so why can't viewers witness the ravaging effect of a real disease on a real sufferer? That, the television censors have decided, is too disturbing for the public to handle.

A Shocking Video and a Shocking Disease

"Sarah's Story" is shocking but so is ALS. The advert is 90 seconds of powerful, disturbing imagery. It opens as a young woman walks into a room and is confronted by a wheelchair. As she gazes questioningly at it, a steel door behind her slams shut. Her body is immediately smashed against a wall. Struggling for breath, she is tossed around the room like a rag doll and left thrashing on the floor. Her clothes are stripped off by an unseen force, and her limbs, twisted and thin, convulse uncontrollably. In the final scene, she sits slumped in the wheelchair, unable to speak or move. However, Clearcast claims that "even good-cause advertising is capable of causing widespread general offense."

I feel that a graphic representation is the only way to ensure that more people are made aware of the horrific physical and emotional impact of ALS. The ban makes me feel as though ALS sufferers must be hidden away. Making the video was tough but so very, very worthwhile. I am extremely proud of it. And I'm afraid the only way to relay the true horror of ALS is in a shockingly vivid way. In fact, the film doesn't really convey the reality of this disease. The reality is far, far worse.

Just after being diagnosed, I spent three years wishing I were dead. Now, I spend every day being thankful that I am not. I am grateful for every moment with my children, although I do wish I could do more with them. My greatest wish is to be around to see them grow up. I am not ashamed to have ALS; I am just different now. I strongly believe that more awareness of ALS can help lead to a cure, and I will continue trying to raise awareness for as long as possible.

GLOSSARY

augmentative and alternative communication (AAC)
Aids such as picture-and-symbol boards and electronic devices used for communication by patients who are unable to write or speak normally.

bulbar muscles
The muscles that control speech, chewing, and swallowing.

Charcot's disease (*maladie de Charcot*)
A name often used for ALS in France, referring to the French neurologist who first described it.

classical ALS
A progressive neurological disease characterized by a deterioration of both upper and lower motor nerve cells (neurons). This type of ALS affects over two-thirds of all people with ALS.

cognitive dysfunction
Difficulty with thinking, memory, or concentration, previously thought not to occur in ALS but now known to affect some ALS patients.

contractures
A shortening of muscles, limiting range of movement and often causing pain.

dysarthria
Impaired speech and language due to weakness or stiffness in the muscles used for speaking.

dysphagia
Impaired chewing and swallowing.

dyspnea
Shortness of breath.

electromyogram (EMG)
An electrical test of muscle function.

El Escorial diagnostic criteria
A set of criteria for determining eligibility for ALS clinical trials.

enteral feeding	Feeding through a tube inserted into the stomach, either through a nostril for short-term feeding or through a small incision in the abdomen for long-term feeding.
etiology	The scientifically determined cause of a disease; in Britain often spelled *aetiology*.
familial ALS (FALS)	A form of ALS that affects more than one member of the same family. This form accounts for only 5–10 percent of ALS cases in the United States.
fasciculations	Involuntary twitchings of muscles.
gastrostomy tube	A feeding tube inserted directly into the stomach through an incision in the abdomen.
Guamanian (or Western Pacific) ALS	A slightly different form of ALS that occurs in Guam and nearby Pacific Islands.
hyperreflexia	Excessive response of muscle reflexes when a normal stimulus is applied.
hyporeflexia	Weak or absent muscle response when a normal stimulus is applied.
hypotonicity	Decrease or loss of normal muscle tone due to the deterioration of the lower motor neurons.
intubation	Insertion of a tube into the body, such as into the wind pipe to assist breathing.
lower motor neurons	Nerve cells (neurons) situated in the spinal cord and brain stem and their projections (axons) forming nerves that end in the muscle fibers.
motor neuron	A neuron that controls a muscle.
motor neuron diseases	A group of disorders in which motor nerve cells (neurons) in the spinal cord and brain stem deteriorate and die. ALS is the most common motor neuron disease.

motor neurone disease (MND)	The name (and spelling) used for ALS in Great Britain and Europe.
muscle atrophy	Loss of muscle fiber volume, resulting in a visible decrease in muscle size. In ALS this occurs because muscles no longer receive impulses, or "messages," from nerve cells (neurons).
muscle cramps	Involuntary, painful shortening of muscles. Often a knotting of the muscles is visible.
myalgia	Muscle pain.
nervous system	The network of specialized cells called neurons, including the brain, that coordinate the processes of the body and transmit signals between its different parts.
neurodegenerative disease	A disease that breaks down tissue in the nervous system. ALS is one of many such diseases.
neurologist	A physician who specializes in diagnosis and treatment of diseases of the nervous system.
neuron	A nerve cell.
neurotransmitter	A chemical that transmits signals from a neuron to another neuron, muscle, or other tissue.
palliative care	Medical care having the goal of minimizing the severity and/or discomfort associated with a disease rather than of curing it.
physician-assisted suicide (PAS)	Suicide of a terminally ill person by means of a drug prescribed but not administered by a physician. This is legal in the states of Oregon, Washington, and Montana and in several European countries.
primary lateral sclerosis (PLS)	A rare form of ALS in which only the upper motor neurons (nerve cells) deteriorate.
progressive bulbar palsy (PBP)	A form of ALS that starts with difficulties speaking, chewing, and swallowing. This disorder affects about 25 percent of people with ALS. Some neurologists consider it a separate disease.

progressive muscular atrophy (PMA)	A form of ALS that starts with deterioration of the lower motor neurons (nerve cells). If the upper motor neurons are not affected within two years, the disease usually remains a lower motor neuron disease.
pseudobulbar affect (PBA)	Involuntary sudden and frequent episodes of laughing or crying unrelated to emotion, often occurring in ALS and other neurological diseases.
riluzole (Rilutek®)	The first drug approved in the United States for the treatment of ALS.
sialorrhea	Drooling resulting from the lack of spontaneous, automatic swallowing to clear excessive saliva in the mouth.
SOD (superoxide dismutase)	An enzyme, the gene for which (SOD1) is the first one found that contains mutations relating to FALS. Defects in this gene account for about 20 percent of FALS cases.
spasticity	Increased muscle tension when the muscle is lengthened, often involving an exaggeration of the tendon reflexes.
spinal muscular atrophy (SMA)	A hereditary neurological disease in which only the lower motor nerve cells are affected.
sporadic ALS (SALS)	ALS that is not inherited and appears without a known cause. This is the most common form of ALS.
statin drugs	Drugs commonly used to lower cholesterol, a treatment thought by most physicians to lower the risk of heart attack. Some doctors believe that these drugs can occasionally cause ALS.
tracheostomy	A surgical operation that creates an opening in the trachea (windpipe) into which a tube to assist breathing is inserted. The term also refers to the opening created.
tracheotomy	An incision into the trachea, or windpipe, usually to assist breathing.

upper motor neurons	Neurons (nerve cells) originating in the brain's motor cortex and their projections (axons) descending through the brain stem and spinal cord.
ventilation	Machine-assisted breathing.
ventilator	A machine that mechanically moves breathable air into and out of the lungs for a patient who is physically unable to breathe. Ventilators may be either noninvasive, using a mask to temporarily deliver oxygen, or invasive, requiring insertion of a tube through the throat called a tracheostomy.
voluntary muscle	A muscle that can normally be controlled by conscious thought. Usually ALS affects only the voluntary muscles.

CHRONOLOGY

1869   French neurologist Jean-Martin Charcot first describes ALS in scientific literature.

1874   Charcot, in a series of lectures based on twenty cases and five autopsies, names the disease amyotrophic lateral sclerosis and establishes it as a clinical entity.

1881   Charcot's paper "On Amyotrophic Lateral Sclerosis" is translated into English and included in a three-volume edition of *Lectures on the Diseases of the Nervous System.*

1883   French neurologist Joseph Jules Dejerinne relates Progressive Bulbar Palsy (PBP) to ALS.

1939   The American public becomes aware of ALS when baseball legend Lou Gehrig's career and, two years later, his life is ended by the disease. He gives his famous farewell speech on July 4.

1950s   The Muscular Dystrophy Association is formed to combat neuromuscular diseases, and Eleanor Gehrig, Lou's widow, becomes its national campaign chairman in order to raise funds for ALS research.

1950s   An ALS epidemic occurs among the Chamorro people on Guam.

1963   Stephen Hawking is diagnosed with ALS. He nevertheless becomes a world-renowned scientist and, as of 2012, has lived longer with the disease than any other person.

1980s   Electronic augmentative and alternative communication (AAC) devices become available to ALS patients who are unable to write or speak normally.

1985   The ALS Association, a national nonprofit patient advocacy group, is founded.

1991   Researchers link chromosome 21 to inherited, or familial, ALS (FALS).

1993   The SOD1 gene on chromosome 21 is found to play a role in some cases of FALS. It is the first gene to be associated with ALS.

1994   The first mice genetically engineered to have ALS are developed for use in research.

1996   Rilutek becomes the first government-approved drug for treating ALS. It is extremely costly and lengthens life by only two or three months.

1998   Criteria for classifying ALS patients in clinical research are developed by the El Escorial World Federation of Neurology.

2009   The first government-approved trial of treating ALS by injecting stem cells into the spine begins.

2010   A genetic link is found between the familial and sporadic forms of ALS.

ORGANIZATIONS TO CONTACT

The editors have compiled the following list of organizations concerned with the issues debated in this book. The descriptions are derived from materials provided by the organizations. All have publications or information available for interested readers. The list was compiled on the date of publication of the present volume; the information provided here may change. Be aware that many organizations take several weeks or longer to respond to inquiries, so allow as much time as possible.

ALS Association
1275 K St. NW, Ste. 1050, Washington, DC 20005
(202) 407-8580
fax: (202) 289-6801
e-mail: advocacy@alsa-national.org
website: www.alsa.org

The ALS Association is the preeminent nonprofit ALS organization and leads the way in global research, providing assistance for people with ALS through a nationwide network of chapters, coordinating multidisciplinary care through certified clinical care centers, and fostering government partnerships. Its website contains extensive information about the disease, plus stories of patients and several downloadable manuals on aspects of living with ALS.

ALS Hope Foundation
1333 Race St., Ste. 202, Philadelphia, PA 19107
(215) 568-2426
website: www.alshopefoundation.org

The mission of the ALS Hope Foundation is to provide long-term support to basic and clinical research programs leading to a cure, clinical centers for the care and treatment of patients with ALS, and support programs for patients and caregivers that optimize care and promote independence for the patient. Among other projects, it funds clinical research and education at the nationally acclaimed MDA/ALS Center of Hope at the Drexel University College of Medicine. Its website contains information about the center as well as about ALS, its possible causes, treatment, and clinical trials.

ALS Society of Canada/ALS411: Youth Peer Support
3000 Steeles Ave. E., Ste. 200, Markham, ON L3R 4T9 Canada
(800) 267-4257
fax: (905) 248-2019
e-mail: alix.shana4als @gmail.com
website: www.als411.ca

This section of the ALS Society of Canada's website, available in both English and French, provides information and support for teens whose parents have been diagnosed with ALS. It offers facts about ALS, personal stories of teens, and a downloadable booklet *When Your Parent Has ALS: A Booklet for Teens.* There is also an associated Facebook group called KALS (Kids of ALS).

ALS Therapy Development Institute (ALS TDI)
215 First St., Cambridge, MA 02142
(617) 441-7200
fax: (617) 441-7299
e-mail: info@als.net
website: www.als.net

ALS TDI is a nonprofit organization with the goal of developing effective therapeutics that stop ALS as soon as possible. Its laboratory, supported by donations, is the leading drug discovery program for ALS. Its website offers information about its research, news about ALS, and forums for the exchange of information about treatments and scientific advances. In addition it is a gateway to a network of over 225 web pages built by members of the ALS community. It also has a Facebook page, YFALS (Young Faces of ALS), for those diagnosed before age thirty.

International Alliance of ALS/MND Associations
e-mail: alliance@alsmn dalliance.org
website: www.alsmnd alliance.org

The International Alliance of ALS/MND Associations provides a forum for support and the exchange of information among more than fifty national patient support and advocacy groups from over forty countries. Its website contains news; policy statements on subjects such as patient rights, good practice in drug trials, genetic testing, and alternative treatments; and a library of downloadable documents about ALS.

Les Turner ALS Foundation
5550 W. Touhy Ave., Ste. 302, Skokie, IL 60077
(888) 257-1107
fax: (847) 679-9109
e-mail: info@lesturner als.org
website: www.lesturn erals.org

The Les Turner ALS Foundation, one of the nation's largest independent ALS organizations, is a local, national, and international leader in research, patient care, and education about ALS, serving more than 90 percent of the ALS population in the Chicago area. It conducts an annual ALS Walk4Life and other events to raise funds and public awareness. Its website contains information about its services and the current issue of its e-newsletter.

Muscular Dystrophy Association (MDA)
3300 E. Sunrise Dr., Tucson, AZ 85718
(800) 344-4863
e-mail: mda@mdausa .org
website: www.als-mda .org

The MDA is a nonprofit health agency dedicated to curing muscular dystrophy, ALS, and related diseases by funding worldwide research, supporting more research on neuromuscular diseases than any other private-sector organization in the world. It also provides comprehensive health care and support services, advocacy, and education. The ALS section of its website contains detailed information plus many downloadable publications, including current and back issues of *Quest* magazine, the *MDA/ALS Newsletter*, and guides to living with ALS.

National Institute of Neurological Disorders and Stroke (NINDS)
PO Box 5801, Bethesda, MD 20824
(301) 496-5751
toll-free: (800) 352-9424
website: www.ninds.nih .gov/disorders/asperg er/asperger.htm

This government institute, part of the National Institutes of Health, researches diseases such as ALS. The institute publishes numerous fact sheets that can be obtained through its website or by contacting the institute directly.

Prize4Life
10 Cambridge Center,
Cambridge, MA 02142
(617) 500-7527
e-mail: contact@prize
4life.org
website: www.prize
4life.org

Prize4Life is a nonprofit organization dedicated to accelerating the discovery of treatments and a cure for ALS by offering prizes, sometimes as much as $1 million, to attract new researchers and drive innovation. Its website contains information about past winners and their achievements as well as competitions now open. It also includes a blog focused on research news and stories of ALS patients.

Project A.L.S.
3960 Broadway, Ste.
420, New York, NY
10032
(800) 603-0270
fax: (212) 420-7387
e-mail: info@project
als.org
website: www.project
als.org

Project A.L.S. is a nonprofit organization aiming to recruit the world's finest scientists and clinicians to work together, rationally and aggressively, toward an understanding of and the first effective treatments for ALS. It supports research in four basic areas: genetics, drug screening, stem cells, and disease pathways. Its website contains information about these areas and an archive of its past newsletters.

FOR FURTHER READING

Books

Bethany Bradsher and Keith LeClair, *Coaching Third: The Keith LeClair Story*. Houston: Whitecaps Media, 2010.

Philip Carlo, *The Killer Within: In the Company of Monsters*. New York: Overlook, 2011.

Jonathan Eig, *Luckiest Man: The Life and Death of Lou Gehrig*. New York: Simon & Schuster, 2006.

Christine Larsen, *Stephen Hawking: A Biography*. Amherst, NY: Prometheus, 2007.

Hiroshi Mitsumoto, ed., *Amyotrophic Lateral Sclerosis: A Guide for Patients and Families*. New York: Demos Health, 2009.

Jozanne Moss and Michael Wenham, *I Choose Everything: Embracing Life in the Face of Terminal Illness*. Grand Rapids, MI: Monarch, 2010.

Augie Nieto and T.R. Pearson, *Augie's Quest: One Man's Journey from Success to Significance*. New York: Bloomsbury, 2007.

David Oliver, Gian Domenico Borasio, and Declan Walsh, eds., *Palliative Care in Amyotrophic Lateral Sclerosis: From Diagnosis to Bereavement*. New York: Oxford University Press, 2006.

David Oliver, *Motor Neurone Disease: A Family Affair*. London: Sheldon, 2011.

Robert E. Paulson, *Not in Kansas Anymore: A Memoir of the Farm, New York City and Life with ALS*. Winnipeg, MB: Gemma B., 2009.

Katrina Robinson, ed., *ALS: Lou Gehrig's Disease Patient Advocate*. Riverside, CA: HealthScouter/Equity, 2009.

Morrie Schwartz, *Morrie: In His Own Words; Life Wisdom from a Remarkable Man*. New York: Walker, 2008.

Kevin Talbot and Rachael Marsden, *Motor Neuron Disease (The Facts)*. New York: Oxford University Press, 2008.

David Tank, *River of Hope: My Journey with Kathy in Search of Healing from Lou Gehrig's Disease*. Menomonie, WI: Planert Creek, 2008.

Darcy Wakefield, *I Remember Running: The Year I Got Everything I Ever Wanted—and ALS*. Cambridge, MA: Da Capo, 2006.

Periodicals and Internet Sources

Nicholas Bakalar, "First Mention: Lou Gehrig's Disease," *New York Times*, October 20, 2009.

Dudley Clendinen, "The Good Short Life," *New York Times*, July 9, 2011.

Disabled-World.com, "Stephen Hawking, A Journey Through Life," March 23, 2010. www.disabled-world.com/editorials /stephen-hawking.php.

Claudia Dreifus, "Life and the Cosmos, Word by Painstaking Word," *New York Times*, May 9, 2011.

EurekAlert, "Boston Univ., Veterans Affairs Find Sports Brain Trauma May Cause Disease Mimicking ALS," August 17, 2010. www.eurekalert.org/pub_releases/2010-08/bumc-buv081710 .php.

————, "Malfunctioning Gene Associated with Lou Gehrig's Disease Leads to Nerve-Cell Death in Mice," January 5, 2011. www.eurekalert.org/pub_releases/2011-01/uops-mga010511 .php.

————, "New Guidelines Identify Best Treatments to Help ALS Patients Live Longer, Easier," October 12, 2009. www .eurekalert.org/pub_releases/2009-10/aaon-ngi100609.php.

————, "New Study Suggests ALS Could Be Caused by a Retrovirus," March 2, 2011. www.eurekalert.org/pub_releases /2011-03/jhmi-nss030211.php.

————, "Researchers Genetically Link Lou Gehrig's Disease in Humans to Dog Disease," January 21, 2009. www.eurekalert .org/pub_releases/2009-01/uom-rg1012109.php.

————, "Smoking May Now Be Considered an Established Risk Factor for ALS, Also Known as Lou Gehrig's Disease," November 16, 2009. www.eurekalert.org/pub_releases/2009-11/bmc -smn111609.php.

————, "UMMS Researchers Isolate First 'Neuroprotective' Gene in Patients with Amyotrophic Lateral Sclerosis," May 11, 2009. www.eurekalert.org/pub_releases/2009-05/uomm -uri051109.php.

John Flowers, "Local Woman Went to Oregon to End Own Life," *Addison County (VT) Independent*, March 10, 2011. www.ad disonindependent.com/2011031ocal-woman-went-oregon-end -own-life.

Michael Gagner, "Finding My Second Wind," *Bakersfield Californian*, September 19, 2009. www.bakersfield.com/opinion/com munity/x746310554/Finding-my-second-wind.

Wes D. Gehring, "Everybody Loves Lou (and Coop, Too): *The Pride of the Yankees*, with Populist Prototype Gary Cooper Playing Lou Gehrig, the Iconic Iron Horse, Still Has the Ability to Make Grown Men Cry." *USA Today* (magazine), September 2010.

Denise Grady, "Veterans Gain U.S. Benefits for Lou Gehrig's Disease," *New York Times*, September 23, 2008.

Amy Harmon, "Fighting for a Last Chance at Life," *New York Times*, May 16, 2009.

International Musician, "Mann Brothers Find Their Way Home," May 2010.

Juliana Keeping, "Planned Research into Lou Gehrig's Disease Could Let Patients Bank Own Stem Cells for Treatment," Ann Arbor.com, November 5, 2010. www.annarbor.com/news /planned-research-into-lou-gerhigs-disease-could-result-in -patients-banking-own-stem-cells-for-treatm/.

Christine Lennon, "The Life-Threatening Disease Women Aren't Supposed to Get," *Marie Claire*, March 2011. www.marieclaire .com/health-fitness/news/als-disease-in-women.

Gretchen Morgenson, "From an Idea by Students, a Million-Dollar Charity," *New York Times*, November 11, 2009.

Chris Museller, "Unforeseen Change of Course for Ailing Sailor," *New York Times*, February 9, 2008.

NewsRx Health, "New Treatment Helps Control Involuntary Crying and Laughing—Common in MS, ALS Patients," May 2, 2010.

NewsRx Health & Science, "Cigarette Smoking Associated with Increased Risk of Developing ALS," March 6, 2011.

Joe O'Connor, "'There Are Too Many Things That Can Be Done,'" *National Post*, April 23, 2011. www.nationalpost.com /news/There+many+things+done/4662541/story.html.

Michael O'Donnell, "Solitary Confinement: Tony Judt Thought a Great Deal About Dignity. His Final Book, Written While the Author Was Dying of ALS, Is the Epitome of It," *Washington Monthly*, January/February 2011. www.washingtonmonthly.com /features/2011/1101.odonnell.html.

Ray Robinson, "70 Years Later, Gehrig's Speech Still Resonates with Inspiration," *New York Times*, June 27, 2009.

Alan Schwartz, "Study Says Brain Trauma Can Mimic A.L.S.," *New York Times*, August 18, 2010.

George Vecsey, "Gehrig's Voice Echoes in a Story of Courage," *New York Times*, July 4, 2009.

Bina Venkataraman, "$1 Million to Inventor of Tracker for A.L.S.," *New York Times*, February 3, 2011.

INDEX

A

ALS Association, 86
ALS patients
    experimental stem cell treatment is
        dangerous for, 70–74
    experimental stem cell treatment may
        benefit, 65–69
    may seek physician-assisted suicide,
        44–52
    personalities of, 76–77
    prevalence of former head injury among,
        56
Amyotrophic lateral sclerosis (ALS, Lou
    Gehrig's disease)
    areas unaffected by, 49
    causes of, 17–19
    early-onset, may be caused by blows to
        head, 53–57
    exercise may slow progression of, 85–88
    experimental stem cell treatment is
        unethical/dangerous in, 70–74
    genetic link between inherited/non-
        inherited forms of, 39–42
    may be caused by severe emotion
        repression, 75–84
    moderate obesity may improve survival
        in, 89–93
    origin of name, 21
    percentage of cases inherited, 13
    percent of cases with hereditary link, 110
    personal account of author's struggle
        with, 115–120
    personal account of Stephen Hawkings'
        life with, 99–105
    personal account of teenage couple
        facing, 106–114
    personal account of woman making ALS
        TV public service ad about, 121–124
    prevalence/annual number of diagnoses
        of, *62, 67, 97*
    prognosis of, 17, 24, 82
    regions with high incidence of, 96
    risk among military veterans, 54
    statin drugs do not increase risk of, 94–97
    technology enables affected people to
        interact with the world, 30–38, 122
    trauma/ TDP-43 and, 58–64
    types of, 19
    warning signs of, *81*
    well-known victims of, 90
Annuls of Neurology (journal), 40
Appel, Stanley H., 58
Autopsy, hallmark of ALS at, 60
Avigan, Mark, 97

B

Bedlack, Richard, 109
Body mass index (BMI), as predictor of
    survival in ALS, 91–92
Boulis, Nicholas, 68
Brain-computer interfaces, 31
Breed, Allen G., 106
Brooks, Rich, 12
Bulbar muscles, *18*

C

Chronic traumatic encephalopathy (CTE),
    59

Conley, John, 66
Contractures, muscle 21
Coppola, Lori, 12
Cresswell, Donna, 122
CTE (chronic traumatic encephalopathy), 59
Cwik, Valerie A., 58

D
Dance, Amber, 89
Day, John W., 58
Diagnosis, 20, 60
    average life expectancy following, 32,
        66–67
Dobel, J. Patrick, 53
Dupuis, Luc, 90, 92

E
Easter, Catherine, 31
Eddowes, Andy, 30–31, 32, 34–35, 37–38
Electromyogram (EMG), 20, 109
End-of-life care, 51–52
    prevalence of ALS patients having
        discussed/made decisions on, 49–50
End-of-life issues, triggers for discussion
    with ALS patients, 47
Euthanasia, 46–48
Exercise
    effect on lifespan in mice with ALS, 88
    may slow progression of ALS, 85–88
Ezekiel, Sarah, 121

F
Fallon, L. Fleming, Jr., 16
Food and Drug Administration, U.S.
    (FDA), 95
Frontotemporal dementia (FTD), 59
FUS gene/protein, 40, 41

G
Gehrig, Lou, 12–13, 15, 53–54, 77–79

Gender, incidence of ALS and, 62, 66, 97
Genetics
    in link between inherited/non-inherited
        forms of ALS, 39–42
    linked with environmental factors in
        cause of ALS, 60
    percentage of ALS cases attributable to,
        13
Glass, Jonathan, 66, 69
Glutamate, 18, 21, 25
Good death, definition of, 52
Gribben, John, 83
Gumbel, Bryant, 54

H
Han-Xiang Deng, 42
Hawking, Stephen, 11–12, 78, 82–83, 99
Head trauma
    association with ALS has not been found,
        61–63
    history of, prevalence among ALS
        patients, 56
    impact-related, 61
    may cause Lou Gehrig's disease, 53–57
Hobbs-Birnie, Lisa, 78, 79, 81
Hospice care, 29, 51
    percentage of ALS patients in showing
        interest in hastening death, 48–49
Hurly, Jane, 85

J
Johnston, Wendy, 44
Jones, Kelvin, 86
Judt, Tony, 115

K
Kafka, Franz, 119
Kurland, Ken, 61

L
Loftus, Mary J., 65

Lou Gehrig's disease. *See* Amyotrophic
   lateral sclerosis

M
Mason, David, 104
Maté, Gabor, 75
McKee, Ann, *55*, 55–57
Melton, Lorna Kay, 108
Melton, Melissa Kay, 108
The Memory Chalet (Judt), 115–120
Metamorphosis (Kafka), 119
Motor neurons, 11, 17, *41*, 69
   degeneration of, effects on muscles, *67*
Muscle & Nerve (journal), 89–90
Muscles
   affected by ALS, *23*
   bulbar, *18*
   contractures of, 21
   effect of motor neuron degeneration on,
      67
   fast-twitch, 86–88
   measurement of deterioration in, *91*
   skeletal, normal *vs.* wasted, *33*
Muscular Dystrophy Association, 22

N
National Institute of Neurological
   Disorders and Stroke (NINDS), 25
National Institutes of Health (NIH), 52
Nelson, Lorene, 61, 62, 97
Neuralstem Inc., 71–73
NIH (National Institutes of Health), 52
NINDS (National Institute of Neurological
   Disorders and Stroke), 25
Nutrition, 22, 27

O
Obama, Barack, 68
Opinion polls. *See* Surveys

P
Paddock, Catherine, 94
Paganoni, Sabrina, 90
Parker, Noland, 108
Parker, Sabrina Kay, 106–114
Paul, Maria, 39
PBA (pseudobulbar affect), 77
Pharmacoepidemiology and Drug Safety
   (journal), 95
Physical therapy, 26
Physician-assisted suicide (PAS), 46–48
   in the Netherlands, 49
   persistent requests for, 51
Polak, Meraida, 66
Polls. *See* Surveys
Pseudobulbar affect (PBA), 77
Psychophysiology (journal), 37

R
Ride for Life, 122
Riluzole (Rilutek), 21, 25–26, 88
Rodriguez, Sue, 77, 79–81
Rutkove, Seward, 91

S
"Sarah's Story" (TV public service ad), 123
Scandone, Nick, 12
Schwartz, Morrie, 77
Scozzari, Audrey, 110
Scozzari, Matt, 107, 109, 110–114, *113*
Siddique, Teepu, 42
Simpson, Elizabeth, 30
Smith, Steve, 57
SOD1 (superoxide dismutase type 1) gene,
   18, 19, 40, 41, 42
Speech/swallowing difficulties,
   management of, 21
Speech therapy, 27
Statins, do not raise risk of ALS, 94–97

Stem cells
  fetal, moral objections to research on, 71, 74
  fetal blood, *68*
  types used for research, *72*
Stem cell treatment, experimental
  is unethical/dangerous, 70–74
  may benefit ALS patients, 65–69
Stephen Hawking, A Life in Science (White and Gribben), 83
Superoxide dismutase type 1 (SOD1) gene, 18, 19, 40, 41, 42
Support groups, 22
Surveys
  of doctors on morphine use, 52
  of neurologists on requests for assisted suicide, 47
  on physician-assisted suicide, 49
Symptoms, 19–20, 116
  treatments for relief of, 26–28

T
TAR DNA-binding protein (TDP43) gene, 40, 59, 63
Tau protein, 59, 63

Taylor, Rebecca, 70
TDP43 (TAR DNA-binding protein) gene, 40, 59, 63
Technology
  enables people with ALS to interact with the world, 11–12, 30–38
  Stephen Hawkings' use of, 104–105
Treatment(s), 21–22, 25–29
  late-stage, 28–29
  for relief of symptoms, 26–28
Tuesdays with Morrie (Albom), 76

U
Urroz, Carlos, 35, 36

V
Veldink, J.F., 49
Ventilation, mechanical, 22, 27, 28–29

W
White, Michael, 83
Wilbourn, Asa J., 76
Wilde, Jane, 102
Wills, Anne-Marie, 90, 92, 93
Woltosz, Walt, 104